Second Ed.

MW00377636

What To Say When

A Guide to More Effective Communication

Rachel Leeds
Esther Wedner
Bernice Bloch

KENDALL/HUNT PUBLISHING COMPANY
4050 Westmark Drive   Dubuque, Iowa 52002

WHAT TO SAY WHEN was generated from the workshop materials which Esther (my dear sister) and I created for our consulting firm Effective Communication Associates. Our insights were gleaned from the research, teaching and writings of many teachers. We mention with great appreciation: Haim Ginott, Jack Gibb, Thomas Gordon, Carl Rogers, Virginia Satir, Philip Zimbardo.

This book is dedicated to courageous and generous Bernice Bloch. Our friend suffered and finally succumbed to the agonies of a crippling illness. She drew comfort and strength from participation in this project. Thank you, dearest friend, for your consistent, helpful presence, your critical listening and your facility with the word.

Rachel Leeds

CONTENTS

ABOUT THE AUTHORS

RACHEL LEEDS

Speech Professor Rachel Leeds of Los Angeles Mission College strikes "pay dirt" at semester's end when she receives cards, letters, gifts and speeches from students. "You have given me the key to finding myself. You taught me that treasure lies in each of us. You had a great influence on all of us." Her passionate mission in the classroom is to transmit her basic premise: "You can enhance the quality of *your* life when you change the How and the Way of your verbal and non-verbal messages." It is to this end that she writes this How-To book with Esther Wedner and Bernice Bloch. Rachel holds an M.Ed and an M.A. in Speech Communications.

ESTHER Y. WEDNER

Esther Wedner earned a Masters in Education in counseling education from the University of Pittsburgh. As counselor and instructor in a school of nursing in a large county hospital in Pennsylvania, she taught communication skills to hundreds of student nurses and other medical personnel. "My extensive experience included teaching interpersonal skills in varied agencies and organizations in the community. As an associate in Effective Communications Associates, I have co-authored and presented with Rachel Leeds a variety of human relations seminars which encompass the skills dealt with in our book." Esther holds certificates in Assertiveness Training, Parent Effectiveness Training and Change Process.

BERNICE BLOCH

Author, teacher and counselor Bernice Bloch counseled adults and children for many years. Her broad teaching experience encompassed work with emotionally troubled youths and the English courses for adults. Her prolific writings included training manuals for school and industry, advertising copy for major retailers, current popular lively and relevant texts for English as a Second Language adult students, inspirational articles and poetry. "I have written poetry, fiction and non-fiction. This book is the culmination of many years of helping students to communicate more effectively." Bernice held an M.A. in Special Education.

INTRODUCTION

In much the same way that a book on carpentry tells the reader how to build a table, with concrete details as to methods and tools, we have developed a simple guide that does the same for building communication skills. We explain the skills; we give easy to follow directions. Our sample dialogues model the techniques for the reader.

Other books tell why communication is so important in the home, in social settings, or in the work place. They explain; they advise, they propose. But they may not tell you what to do and *how* to do it.

When a patient comes to the doctor with chest pain, the doctor knows why he must check out several possible problem areas. The tools that he uses are the stethoscope and a cardiogram. He thumps on the patient's chest and obtains oral information, among other procedures. He knows why and he knows how.

When a woman needs to change her cooking habits because she wants to lose weight, she knows why she has to omit fats, salts, sugars and oils from her diet. She buys the vegetables, the steamer, the teflon pots, and the getting thin cookbooks. She knows why and she knows how.

What to Say When emphasizes HOW TO rather than WHY. Most of us know why we would like to communicate more effectively but we don't know how! Here's the HOW TO!

Our books will tell you:

- How to change the conversation you have inside your own head so that you can change communication habits that don't work for you.

- How to make connections with new people easily.

- How to recognize your listening habits and improve them so that you understand others and they feel valued and heard.

- How to meet a problem situation with a sense of your own ability to handle it effectively.

- How to create an atmosphere of openness and

trust rather than one of defensiveness and distrust.

Equipped with the how to's, with conscious effort and practice, you will be able to modify the way you talk and listen to others. For instance, when your newly divorced friend shares her anguish and loneliness, instead of giving her advice, which she doesn't want, you will listen intently and reflect back her sense of overwhelming loss which you perceive. Your friend will feel comforted by your non-judgmental understanding.

You'll also learn to cope more effectively with some of your problems by honestly and objectively describing them instead of suffering in silence. For example, if your mom calls you several times a day, sometimes at the most inappropriate hour, you will be able to tell her in a tactful, careful message that when you have to answer the phone in the midst of dinner or the first thing in the morning before you've brushed your teeth, that you're too preoccupied to give her the attention she needs. Your manner and your message will help her understand your problem.

We all want to be liked and understood. When we communicate to achieve understanding and to show our respect for others, positive changes occur in the flow of our relationships. There will be more honesty, trust and acceptance. Your communication moves your relationships - up or down, backwards or forward. You make the choice!

WHAT TO SAY WHEN

A GUIDE TO MORE EFFECTIVE
COMMUNICATION

"ARE YOU AFRAID TO CHANGE"?

Chapter 1

Rachel Leeds

Esther Wedner

Bernice Bloch

ARE YOU AFRAID TO CHANGE?

WHAT TO SAY WHEN . . .

. . . The old ways don't work for you and you're scared of making changes.

Sherry is wearing her red, trendy outfit to the "Let's Get Together" party at the management conference. She thinks she looks smashing; yet her inner quakings reflect her anxiety.

Sherry:

I don't know a soul in this room. Why did I come?

There's a nice looking guy at the bar. He seems to be checking out the territory, too.

I think I'll go over and introduce myself. What if he ignores me? What will I say to him?

I just can't do this! I could never make small talk! The heck with it; I'll finish my drink and go back to my room.

Trapped by the insistent talk in her head, Sherry feels defeated once more!

WHAT TO SAY WHEN

"Some enchanted evening you will meet a stranger across a crowded room" can come true for you! Are you feeling anxious about the prospect? Well, join the crowd! Even the thought of starting a conversation with a stranger can be frightening for many social introverts.

"Hello, I'm Larry Ashton," may not be so easy to say if Larry is the kind of person who always waits to be introduced. Learning a new skill can cause palpitations or any of a number of symptoms that manifest themselves when we think we need to change.

Change makes cowards of us all! You may argue that your inhibitions, which maintain your status quo, serve you well on many a score. Yes, you can remain indifferent and passive and thus avoid the "should" and "ought" of social convention. Yes, you can wear your mask and always be labeled "meek and timid." But is that how you want to spend the rest of your life? To help you answer these questions, ask yourself:

- Do you often experience loneliness and boredom?

- Do you experience rejection more often than acceptance in your social life?

WHAT TO SAY WHEN

- Do you feel disappointed about the direction of your career?

- Do you feel dissatisfied with your family relationships?

If you've answered "yes" to these questions, you're saying "no" to life's challenges, opportunities and pleasures. On the other hand, if you're willing to make changes, there's a whole world of people out there who can add new dimensions to your life.

If in your past, the world out there seemed hostile, it may be that your lack of social initiative put the burden of relating on others. Consequently, relationships were strained before they started. What did you get? Rejection and loneliness.

If your heart's not in your work, it may be that you see possibilities as fraught with hidden dangers. A promotion to you means more responsibilities. New undertakings speak of doom and dread. Getting to know personnel in the new department may expose your rough edges!

Change doesn't have to make a coward of you. Isn't a promotion a validation of your abilities? Doesn't the new camaraderie of your work place make you want to go to work in the morning? If you believe that the person who can stand in the critical eye of the spotlight, smiling confidently, gets the praise and promotion and perks, you may be right. Couldn't that person be you?

WHAT TO SAY WHEN

Finally, how does it go with the family connection? Feel second-best to your brother? Exploited by your mother? Alienated? Funny, isn't it? You're keeping your mouth shut so that you don't make waves. Moreover, if you're not pulling your own strings, then someone else is jerking you around. And that's no laughing matter. That's sad!

Make some positive changes. We can show you how! Your decision to change will lead to more than making new friends. It will be the beginning of a new approach to life and living. A new way of thinking about yourself and others, a richer and more rewarding way of "being" in the world.

WHAT TO SAY WHEN

COMMUNICATION SELF-EVALUATION

Before reading this book any further, it may be a good idea to check your own patterns of communication. Then you will be able to compare your present responses with those you will make after you have become more aware of the "how-to's" of communication effectiveness.

Score 1-5
(5 being highest)

1.   I can walk into a room and enter a conversation   _____

2.   I feel comfortable in a room full of strangers   _____

3.   I like to express my opinion.   _____

4.   I prefer talking on the phone to talking face-to-face.   _____

5.   I usually know what to say when a friend needs to talk.   _____

6.   I make friends easily.   _____

7.   I can express my feelings.   _____

WHAT TO SAY WHEN

8.   I like to show affection
        to people I care
        about.   _____

9.   I like making small talk.   _____

10.   I can accept a compliment.   _____

11.   I can be assertive.   _____

12.   I can discuss without getting
        into an argument.   _____

13.   I give advice to my friends.   _____

14.   I analyze my friends'
        problems.   _____

15.   I share common problems with
        my friends.   _____

16.   I ask questions about my
        friends' problems.   _____

17.   I show empathy when I listen to
        my friends' problems.   _____

18.   I like to help my friends "keep
        their cool" in traumatic
        situations.   _____

19.   I like to give compliments.   _____

20.   I find it difficult to say
        "no."   _____

WHAT TO SAY WHEN

21.   I often do what I "should" do
            instead of what I want to do.   _____

22.   I'm afraid of disapproval when
            I express a controversial
            opinion.   _____

23.   I don't say what I think or
            feel if my listener will get
            upset.   _____

Problems in relationships occur due to faulty communication patterns. We know we can help you improve. Read on and let us show you how.

WHAT TO SAY WHEN

A GUIDE TO MORE EFFECTIVE
COMMUNICATION

"WHAT ARE YOU SAYING TO YOURSELF"?

Chapter 2

Rachel Leeds

Esther Wedner

Bernice Bloch

WHAT ARE YOU SAYING TO YOURSELF?

WHAT TO SAY WHEN . . .

. . . what you are saying to yourself hurts more than it helps.

Laura has just returned from a date with a new acquaintance, Bill. For weeks her friends had touted Bill as "The Man" for Laura - charming, self-educated, ambitious, handsome. Sadly, the long-awaited date bombs!

Laura is chagrined and despondent. She says to herself:

> **I'll never get fixed up again. I always suffer through these games. I should know better. A single man of 30 must be a loser!**

Laura blocks relationships by what she is saying to herself.

Contemporary psychologists claim that people who suffer high levels of anxiety and other harmful emotions victimize themselves through faulty belief systems. To change, we need to understand our assumptions and how they operate to help or hinder our relationships. We can learn how to

WHAT TO SAY WHEN

turn them around. If you are hesitant about acquiring new skills or improving your relationships, it would help if you listened closely to your own head talk. Self-awareness is the key to self-challenge and change.

To check out your "irrational" beliefs, take this self-talk test:

- Do I catastrophize?
  "It will be just *awful* if I don't have the report ready today. He'll question my promotion."

- Do I over-generalize?
  "Singles places are a drag! I *never* meet anyone worthwhile there."

- Do I cop-out?
  "I *can't* take you to the doctor. I *don't* drive the freeways."

- Do I have to be perfect?:
  "I can't give the report; I haven't had time to edit it again. It's *not good enough!*"

- Do I need everyone's approval?
  "John didn't even smile at my joke; *he doesn't like me.* I'm so embarrassed."

- Do I have to take responsibility for other's behavior?
  "He turned away from me. *I must have come on too strong!*

WHAT TO SAY WHEN

- Do I constantly "should" on myself?
  "I *should* call Mom tonight. She likes to hear from me every week."

If you answered "yes" to any of the above questions, it may be time to challenge your belief system. What you believe is expressed in the sentences which you say to yourself. When you change your beliefs, you modify your HEAD TALK.

WHAT TO SAY WHEN

Do you find yourself:

Catastrophizing:	I'll just die if I don't get this job!
Overgeneralizing:	Everybody's out to get you. They'll con you every time!
Cop-out:	I can't visit you in the hospital. I can't take the whole scene!
Perfectionism:	If you can't do a job right, don't do it at all.
Approval:	I can't face Elena. She said I embarrassed her at the party!
Taking Responsibility:	Mom was so upset with the news. I must have told her the wrong way!
Shoulds:	You shouldn't make your own plans for Thanksgiving. You know we always have dinner together.

Perhaps you can identify some of your own "irrational" head talk in the following examples:

CATASTROPHIZING:

Jennifer agonizes over the expenses of her prom and decides that she can't go. Then she projects a scenario

WHAT TO SAY WHEN

of rejection by her friends: "They won't forgive me and they'll drop me." She forecasts the "worst" and needlessly stresses herself.

OVER-GENERALIZATION:

Karen exaggerates shortcomings and makes a trauma of disappointments.

"You never talk to me."
"You always disappoint me."
"I'm a lousy student. I always procrastinate."
"She's selfish. She never offers to help me."

Words like "always" and "never" define some behavior as a totality that does not vary. Generalizing from a single event to perpetuity doesn't make sense.

Furthermore, over-generalizing makes for inaccurate and harmful beliefs. Sandra says of her sister, "*SHE NEVER HELPS*," failing to consider that sis does help in other ways that Sandra doesn't choose to remember. Consequently, Sandra is needlessly angry. If you say, "I'm always late," you give yourself permission to continue your tardiness. You're choosing not to change.

Awareness of this tendency can help you avoid such reactions.

WHAT TO SAY WHEN

Instead of Saying:	Say:
You never talk to me.	Lately when I ask you what's wrong, you don't answer me.
You always disappoint me.	When you arrive late, I am disappointed.
I'm a lousy student.	I need to change my study habits. I wrote my term paper at the last minute and got a "D" grade.
She never helps me.	She did not help me with tonight's dinner, but she made Christmas dinner for us all.

COP-OUT:

Susan says: "I can't do it," when she has to give a talk in her speech class. Her head talk gives her permission to "cop-out." Susan can acknowledge her deep anxiety while at the same time she reassures herself: "Perhaps I can learn to be less nervous." When she changes her belief in the impossibility of the challenge, she can change.

WHAT TO SAY WHEN

PERFECTIONISM:

Mrs. Jones would like to invite her new neighbor into her new home but it's *missing* some furniture. Never mind the warm comfort of the colors and basic furnishings. Never mind her own loneliness. "When it's finished, I can entertain." She short-changes herself just as Martha does when she won't go to the party because the hairdresser cut her hair too short.

APPROVAL:

Do you need to have everyone pat you on the head and say: "You're great!" "You did good!" "You look so handsome?" If so, poor you! You're trapped by the insatiable need to have everyone's approval for all that you do, and that's impossible. A much easier guiding motif might be: "Win some, lose some."

Otherwise, you'll find yourself in some untenable situations:

- You'll go to see a horror film to please your friend, though you know you'll suffer nightmares.

- You'll join your husband at the local barbecue bistro though you can't stand spareribs.

WHAT TO SAY WHEN

- You'll find yourself in law school to please your parents, though your intuition and preference say: "NO!"

TAKING RESPONSIBILITY:

Arthur is also beset by beliefs which heap guilt and a sense of duty. Each day he calls his mother and finds stories to spice up her dull, dreary existence. Arthur assumes full responsibility for his mother's moods. Deep down he believes that it would be "awful" if he failed his mother. He needs to be the "perfect" son by his mother's definition. So the talk that moves around in his head makes the conflict and dissatisfaction he feels.

Change the head talk, Arthur! You don't have to be the "perfect" son. Those beliefs can go. You can permit mother *to take responsibility* for putting more satisfaction into her own life and still be a concerned son without feeling so burdened and resentful!

SHOULDS:

Picture Matsuko. A second generation Asian American, she sees the stranger across the crowded room and muses:

WHAT TO SAY WHEN

Gee, that guy in the tweed jacket is handsome. I sure would like to talk to him, but he might think I'm brazen.

Heeding parental dictates, Matsuko misses out on a good bet. She might stop "shoulding" on herself, initiate the encounter, and find she is still a genteel lady! Meantime, she breaks the mold created by ancestors long dead.

Yes, indeed, it gets serious when your Head Talk is triggered by any of these fallacious patterns: If you let faulty beliefs determine your behavior, are you leading your own life? Why not be your own person? Change counterproductive habits. How? By changing your Head Talk.

Your "Head Talk" refers to what you say to yourself about whatever is going on in your life. "She'll be mad if I don"t call." "I should go see Mom." Look at the separate statements which make up this inner dialogue. Examine them for faulty beliefs. Are you catastrophizing? Overgeneralizing? Striving for perfection? Looking for approval? Copping out? Taking responsibility? Shoulding? Step back, analyze and decide to change each statement. A more rational thought will create a more productive, less hurtful attitude.

Albert Ellis and adherents of the rational-emotive approach to change recommend that we scrutinize the talks in our head surrounding the troubling situation that causes butterflies in our stomach and tension headaches. Write

WHAT TO SAY WHEN

down the incessant conversation that governs such thoughts. When you write down your Head Talk, give it a hard, searching look.

Remember Laura's date with Bill? Laura is chagrined and despondent. Let's listen to her head talk. She writes each thought, examines it, then writes a new response.

Laura's Self Talk	Laura's Review and New Dialogue
I'll never get fixed up again.	*Never* is a long time. Instead, Laura says, "This is the third time this month that I've been disappointed in a 'match.'"
I always suffer through these games.	I'm *over-generalizing*. It wasn't all bad. I enjoyed the dinner. We had some laughs when I told him about my crazy idea.
If Bill's still single at 35, he must be a loser.	I'm *shoulding*. A man should be married by 36 is unrealistic in today's world when it takes so long to make it professionally.

WHAT TO SAY WHEN

Only a "nerd" would wear white socks.

Perfectionism! I expect every man I date to have the dress code of Mr. Q!

I should have checked him out more carefully.

Should! If I check out every inch of my friends, I'll never get from "A" to "B" because I'll never let a man be himself.

He sure said goodby in a hurry because I didn't invite him in. I made him mad.

Responsibility! I didn't make him mad. He sounded hurt but that's how he chose to feel. His feelings are his choice. I don't feel guilty about saying good night when I did.

As Laura gains more insight into her feelings and beliefs, she sees what she has been doing, and decides to make some changes. She opens the door to new possibilities for her future encounters.

WHAT TO SAY WHEN

Anne has just talked to her daughter Sheryl who has decided to take off for South America with her boyfriend instead of continuing her third year at the University. Anne is beside herself and is distracted from her own graduate studies.

Anne's Self Talk

Anne's Review and Dialogue

The kid hates me. She'll do anything to hurt me.

Sheryl is not running away to get even with me. I'm not responsible; she's got a man in her life.

She's always been impossible.

I'm *over-generalizing*. I remember when she was a typical teenager who refused to wear what I bought her. I had to remember then that I tried to teach her to be her own person.

I hate her guts.

That's altogether irrational. I just hate what she's doing because she's rejecting my *shoulds*.

WHAT TO SAY WHEN

Where did I go wrong?

Perfection and *generalization* again. I was a working mother and spent quality time with my daughter. There's no such thing as a "perfect" mother. I have to stop beating myself because I am not all the things I want to be.

Anne and Laura questioned belief patterns which generated debilitating and counterproductive self-talk. Stepping back and analyzing their Head Talk enabled them to terminate the self-hatred and endless recriminations. They could pick up the pieces again and cope.

Though the recommended procedure is to write your thoughts and their challenges, some of you may prefer to use the tape recorder for the same purpose. Bernice recorded her thoughts and listened to her responses. She found it a very effective means of gaining insight into her considered options. For her, that was the key to making changes.

What we say to ourselves determines what we are going to say to others, whether it's inviting a person to lunch or confronting your partner at brunch. We can dissect our faulty premises and clean up the distressing monologue for an effective and meaningful dialogue.

WHAT TO SAY WHEN

A GUIDE TO MORE EFFECTIVE COMMUNICATION

"HOW DO YOU MAKE NEW FRIENDS"?

Chapter 3

Rachel Leeds

Esther Wedner

Bernice Bloch

HOW DO YOU MAKE NEW FRIENDS?

WHAT TO SAY WHEN . . .

. . . you're in a new place and you want to make new friends and you don't know how.

At the Workout

Jean: Hi, I'm Jean. Are you here for beginner's aerobics?

Don: Hi, Jean. I'm Don. Yes, I am. I just joined the workout. (Free information)

Jean: So did I. I figure it's time to do some for the old bod. (Sharing personal thoughts)

Don: The "old" bod doesn't look old to me, Jean. You look like a size "8." Am I right? (Compliment)

Jean: Thanks, Don. I'm feeling "old" so I figure it's time to do something to renew myself. (Self-disclosure)

Don: Well, exercise does that for you, I hear. It gives you energy and

> makes you feel good. That's why
> I'm here. Now, I just have to stick
> to my resolution to stay with it.

Jean: Well, I guess I'll be seeing you. I
               joined for a year.

Clearly, Jean and Don have learned to make a new connection.

After you have learned to examine your Head Talk you can substitute a new belief system that will keep you growing. With time you will be able to stop worrying about yourself and start concentrating on others. That's a sure-fire way of substituting action for inertia. Take the risk - that first small step! If you want to enlarge your circle of friends, we describe ways to initiate new relationships through your first encounters - your initial communications.

Conversations usually involve a search for mutual interests. The content, be it small talk, exchanging facts or opinions about what's happening, is simply the means we use to find common ground. What is the underlying message? "I'm interested in talking to you. Maybe, you're interested, too. Let's see how it goes." During these first minutes we size each other up to see if we want to keep the ball rolling.

WHAT TO SAY WHEN

When you cross that "crowded room," keep in mind that sometimes it's easier to start a conversation with a stranger. She doesn't know anything about your past history and takes you at face value. If you think of it that way, it makes talking easier. You're not out to impress or compete with gabby George or serious Sarah. And should your opening remark meet with a shunning shoulder, you say to yourself: "That person is either very shy or preoccupied. I'll go over to meet someone else."

The intention, at this time, is not to make a bosom buddy. You just want to meet some new people. So get something going.

WHAT TO SAY WHEN

OPENERS

You can use an opener that hooks into wherever you happen to be. Here are some typical openers. Try some of these:

At a Party

"Great party, isn't it?"

* * *

"This is a lovely home for parties, don't you think?

* * *

At a Singles Social

"Do you like the 50's music?"

* * *

"I notice you can't keep your feet still. My feet want to dance too."

* * *

"This is my first singles party. It took all my courage to come here."

WHAT TO SAY WHEN

"Do you know any of these people?"

At the Travel Club

"I notice you talking to several people. How long have you been a member of this group?"

* * *

"My name is Dorothy. Is this your first time here?"

* * *

"Hi. That travel agent certainly knows some interesting places to go. I'd like to go to Alaska."

At the Supermarket

"I'm just starting to cook with herbs. Could you tell me what to do with basil?"

* * *

"It looks like you're cooking Italian food. All that fancy spaghetti and

WHAT TO SAY WHEN

the tomato sauce reminds me of a
neighbor who loved to make pasta
dishes."

How many times have you avoided small talk
because you just didn't know what to say? A few
times? Many times? More times than you care
to count? You're not alone with this problem. A
frequent comment is. "I just don't like small talk!
It's too shallow." But the truth of the matter may
be that you feel very uncomfortable with strangers when you don't have a ready-made script.
However, help is on the way, so don't give up.

WHAT TO SAY WHEN

LET'S TALK TOPICS

Topics that may seem cliché at other times and places are recognized as perfectly acceptable ways of initially relating to other people. These topics are the tools of the trade when it comes to the area of small talk.

The Weather

"This has been a terrible hot spell! I never dreamed this kind of weather would follow me out to L.A."

The Home Town

"I've just moved here from Columbus. I really like it; people have been so helpful and friendly."

The Family

"Your little girl seems to love the swimming pool. Has she been swimming very long?"

The Work Place

"I see on your name tag that you're in the export division. What do you do?"

WHAT TO SAY WHEN

OFFERING HELP

Another opening gambit is the simple act of offering help. That small action of graciousness is just good manners and takes only a small amount of effort on your part.

At the Party

"May I get you a glass of wine?"

At a Meeting

"I'll pull up a chair for you."

On a Coffee Break

"Can I get you a refill?"

On the Plane

"Would you like to read my newspaper?"

WHAT TO SAY WHEN

ASKING FOR HELP

At the Market

"I see you bought shark. I've never been brave enough to try it. How do you cook it?"

At the Party

"You're certainly a good dancer! Would you show me how to do that step?"

At School

"I missed last week's lecture. Could you tell me what he talked about."

OBSERVATIONS

Still another way to break the ice is to comment on something you've observed. Of course, you'll make only positive comments. Who knows, you may be talking to the host's brother when you're ready to comment that the wine is much too sweet and could only have been bought by a novice.

At the Party

"I see you're eating a cheese ball. How is it? Do you recommend it?"

At the Work Place

"I've seen you in the cafeteria several times and I'm wondering where you work."

At a Social Gathering

"I've been admiring your haircut. Do you mind telling me where you had it done?"

WHAT TO SAY WHEN

COMPLIMENTS

Your openers initiated the conversation. And now, you may ask, where do I go from here? The next step is to compliment your new acquaintance, in a sincere, friendly and appropriate manner. In our society, compliments are too few and far between. William James observed: "The deepest principle in human nature is the craving to be appreciated." Unfortunately, we seem more likely to tell others what's wrong rather than what's right and bright. Our ethics stress modesty and humility to the point where we find it difficult to receive praise.

For the most part, we are prepared to think well of other people. Yet so often we find these positive feelings difficult to express. But who doesn't like a shot of vitamin love? Come on. Let's face it. You do. I do. We all do.

We are like plants that blossom in a warm, sunny environment. Compliments, or strokes, are validation of our uniqueness and, as such, are the sun's rays that touch our souls and make our spirits soar. So, at a party, if you think that a stranger is dressed attractively, why not say so? When you express admiration, you come across as empathetic and attractive. "Say," says he, "I like that red dress you're wearing. I know it sounds corny but it's not just a line. I really mean it."

WHAT TO SAY WHEN

"What," says she, "this old thing? I put it on at the last minute. But thanks, I'm glad you like it." To encourage you to tell others what you admire about them, we want to share Alan Garner's simple formula for delivering "an honest positive."

Be sincere.

Be specific in your description of what you like.

Use the person's name.

Ask a question following your compliment to help the other person feel comfortable with the praise.

First: *Say what you see.* <u>Describe the specific behavior, possession, or quality you admire.</u>

"I like your blue windbreaker. It matches your eyes."

"I notice you eat all the vegetables and pass up the high calorie foods."

"It looks like you have something nice to say to each of the people we've talked to."

Second: *Say the person's name.* <u>It makes them feel special.</u>

WHAT TO SAY WHEN

"Jerry, I like your blue windbreaker. It matches your eyes."

Betty, I notice you eat all the vegetables and pass up the high calorie foods."

"Bill, it seems you have something nice to say to each of the people we've talked to."

Third: *Follow your compliment with a question.* This takes the focus off the person praised. This permits him to acknowledge with "Thanks" and permits him to move easily into answering the question.

Jerry, I like your blue windbreaker. It matches your eyes. Is blue your favorite color?

Betty, I notice you eat all the vegetables and pass up the high calorie food. Are you dieting?

WHAT TO SAY WHEN

ASKING QUESTIONS

Let's add another skill to your social repertoire. If used properly, it will further the relationship. Asking questions can be a boon or a bummer.

Judy:	"How often do you work out?"
Joe:	"Twice a week."
Judy:	"Do you live near here?"
Joe:	*"No."*
Judy:	"Do you live in the valley?"
Joe:	*"No."*
Judy:	"Do you . . ."

Yes, Joe could have been more communicative and might have offered more in the dialogue. But shy people don't often volunteer information because they're afraid what they have to say may not be interesting. Or they might be anxious about meeting new people and are inhibited in their responses.

There is a knack to asking questions without making you sound like Ivan the Inquisitor. If your tone of voice is warm and the smile on your face is friendly, very few people will be offended by your questions. If your attitude intimates "I like you. You seem interesting. I'd like to know more about you," very few people will find your questioning impolite. So, first be sure of your *body language*.

WHAT TO SAY WHEN

Ask questions that require more than a yes/no
answer. Ask an "open" question rather than a
"closed" question. Questions that ask for a "yes"
or "no" or one-word answer close a conversation
or make for stilted replies. Phrase your questions
sos that your partner can say as much as he wants
about the subject. The following examples
illustrate the difference between the open and
closed questions.

Closed Question	Open Ended Question
"Did you like the speaker?"	"What did you think of the speaker at last night's meeting?"
"Are you going away for the holidays?"	"What are your plans for your vacation?"
"Did you like the entertainment on your cruise?"	Tell me about the entertainment on your cruise."
"Have you been having any fun?"	"What've you been doing for fun lately?"
"Do you like being a senior in college?"	"What's it like being a senior in college and facing the real world?"
"Do you like being retired?"	"How do you fill in your time from 9:00 to 5:00 now that you're retired?"

WHAT TO SAY WHEN

Asking an open-ended question does not guarantee a vociferous response, but chances are that your partner will answer with more than one word. That type of question not only asks for elaboration and explanations, but shows that you are interested in continuing the conversation beyond mere fact finding.

Though you may not be accustomed to asking questions in this way, it's a skill, like any other, that requires practice and time. Like handwriting, it becomes automatic.

WHAT TO SAY WHEN

FREE INFORMATION

You can move a conversation along by giving <u>free information</u>. That makes your answers to the open questions more detailed, more complete, more interesting. <u>Free information</u> is simply that part of the conversation that is given, but not required or necessarily expected. The added descriptive words put meat on the bare bones of fact finding. The good conversationalist listens and takes advantage of <u>free information</u> by *commenting on it, asking questions* related to it, or *sharing personal thoughts or opinions through self-disclosure.* With this kind of mutual sharing, the conversation flows. For example:

"How do you like the aerobics class?" (Open question)

"I think the instructors are good, but I hate the music!"(- Free information)

"What's wrong with the music?" (Open question)

"Plenty. First, they play it too loud. They must have hearing loss. And second, I can't stand the rock sound of this generation. I go for light classical and show tunes, some country." (Self disclosure)

In giving *"free information"* you are sharing aspects of yourself and your experience. It tells the listener that you're open and reaching out. Giving information about yourself allows the partner some

insight into you and some conversational hook with
which to continue.

WHAT TO SAY WHEN

SELF-DISCLOSURE

Self-disclosure indicates that you are willing to tell the other person about your interests, your hobbies, your politics, your preferences. Any piece of information that you give freely helps to move the conversation along and may enable you both to find common interest. *Self-disclosure* tells your listener that you want to involve yourself in a mutual openness and reach out for a possible relationship.

"How do you like the way they've changed the market?" (Open question)

"I don't know. After shopping here *for ten years*, I don't know my way around." (Free information)

"You've lived in this neighborhood a long time. (Comment) I just moved here last year. Sometimes I feel overwhelmed by the size of this market. I miss the small, ethnic markets of my old neighborhood." (Self-disclosure)

In response to the open question, the other person offers some free information. You then comment and add to the flow of the dialogue with self-disclosure.

Judy:

Hi, I'm Judy. You must be a new member. *How do you like the health club?*

WHAT TO SAY WHEN

After introducing herself, Judy uses an opener and follows with an <u>open-ended question.</u>

Joe

Oh, I'm getting used to it. *I've been here two months, and my muscles don't ache anymore.*

Joe responds to the question and offers some <u>free information.</u>

Judy

Great! Yes, I know what you mean. I joined a year ago and boy, do they give you a workout. Which exercise do you like best?

Judy responds by commenting on Joe's <u>free information.</u> <u>Self-disclosure</u> permits Judy to share with Joe how long he has been a member and to agree with his feelings about the strain of the workout. She follows with another <u>open-ended</u> question.

Joe

I use the Nautilus equipment but I really like aerobics.

Judy

I see, you work out on the gym's machines but aerobics is more fun for you.

WHAT TO SAY WHEN

WHAT TO SAY WHEN

Judy <u>paraphrases</u> Joe's answers. This tells him she has heard what he said and is interested in hearing more.

Joe

Yes, and I meet some nice people there.

Joe does go on by commenting on the connections he has made, thus <u>complimenting</u> Judy in a roundabout fashion.

Judy

Gee, thanks. I like you too!

If you've tuned in to our message about conversations, you picked up some clues to becoming an "expert." There's no secret, no magical potion, just questions, compliments, free information and self-disclosure.

Let's look in on two women in the university library. Betty is seated at he table, reading a text on art appreciation. Edith, carrying a stack of books, is on her way out. As she passes Betty's table, she stops and speaks.

WHAT TO SAY WHEN

Scene	Explanation
Edith: "Hi, you look familiar. I think we're in the same art class."	Edith takes the risk and approaches the class-mate. She comments on a common interest - the art class.
Betty: "Oh, yes. Hello, I recognize you. I sit behind you and I always admire the way you wear your hair."	Betty responds with a compliment.
Edith: "Well, thank you. I haven't seen you in class lately."	Edith acknowledges the compliment and then notes that she, too, has observed something - Betty's absence.
Betty: "I've had back surgery and I've been out of school for four months."	Betty responds to an implied question with the reason for and the duration of her absence. This is free information offered to Edith.
Edith: "I see you're wearing a brace. How does it feel?"	Edith picks up the free information and com-ments on what she sees and asks an open-ended question about it.

WHAT TO SAY WHEN

Betty: "It's hot and sticky and cumbersome. But it helps me. That's what really counts."

Betty uses self-disclosure as she responds to the question, telling what she feels and thinks about the brace.

Edith: "Well, I have to rush to another class now. But if you want to read my notes, or if I can help, just ask. I'll give you my name and phone number. Oh, I forgot to introduce myself. I'm Edith Walker."

Edith is preparing Betty for her imminent departure. She offers to help Betty. She introduces herself.

Betty: "I'm Betty Stone. Certainly is nice to meet you at last."

Betty responds and introduces herself.

Are you sharing a jacuzzi or hot tub with some of the guys and gals? You want to be friendly without acting like you're "coming on" to someone. Let's examine this interaction and see how sharing a common experience can ease the path to friendship.

WHAT TO SAY WHEN

Scene

Explanation

Jim: "Hi. That jacuzzi looks inviting. I just moved in. Thought I'd relax after unpacking six million boxes."

Jim self-discloses his thoughts about the hot tub. He offers free information. He just moved in and is tired after unpacking six million boxes.

Terry: "Moving is hard work! Come on in. You'll feel better."

Terry responds to the free information and comments on it. Then asks Jim to join them.

Dave: "I sure hope you're kidding about all those boxes."

The third party sharing the jacuzzi also comments on the free information.

Jim: "Well, maybe not six million, but a lot. I collect old records, LPs and stuff from the thirties on up to the break music kids are playing today. I love all kinds of music."

Jim offers an explanation for "six million boxes" and offers more information about himself - his love of music.

Dave: "Are you a musician?"

Dave picks up on Jim's self-disclosure with a question.

Dave: "Yeah, I play the trumpet."

WHAT TO SAY WHEN

Terry: "We sure could have some great parties around here. I play piano. My neighbor plays the guitar. Now we've got a trumpet player! Welcome to Wilshire Square."

Terry shares what they have in common and offers an opportunity to the newcomer for further interaction.

Think of the person in your life who never seems to be at a loss for words. Chances are he's using the very same techniques that you are learning.

PARAPHRASING

This is yet another skill that's commonly used by effective communicators.

<u>Paraphrasing</u> is a conversational catalyst that tells your partner that you are interested, you want to hear more, and you're tuned into her wave length. How do you *paraphrase*? By giving your own version of what the speaker said, by restating in your own words the basic content and feeling expressed.

R: Dan Douglas got out of prison today after five years. He killed the Mayor and a city councilman! Is that justice?

E: *You seem disturbed that he got off so easily for such terrible crimes.*

* * *

B: The meeting seems to go on and on. I don't have time to sit around.

T: *You seem bored and in a hurry to get out.*

* * *

WHAT TO SAY WHEN

J: This PACE instructional program has been a shot in the arm for me. There's more to life than work and the tube!

R: *Sounds like you're really excited about this program!*

* * *

B: I can't find enough hours to work, take care of the kids and keep up with the assignments. I don't need a course in time management. I need four more hours a day!

L: *You seem overwhelmed by all you have to do.*

What is the dynamic here? *Paraphrasing* simply lets your speaker now that you're tuned into what she is saying. You clarify what you hear and show that you understand. Moreover, when you focus on the important parts of the message, you avoid the distractions of your own head talk. Anybody who gets this kind of affirming feedback tends to continue to share his feelings and insights because you've made him feel special! In addition, you find that what you're hearing stretches you also. And you've taken the burden off of yourself to keep the conversation going. *Paraphrasing* is an integral part of good listening habits.

WHAT TO SAY WHEN

People will share more personal information with each other after they find that it is safe to do so. You will find out through small talk and your initial search for mutual interest whether it is comfortable to disclose more than just factual material. If so, you can reveal to each other ideas and opinions, likes and dislikes. You can risk being vulnerable when you have built a foundation of trust. This takes time and careful attention to the need of the other person.

Relationships, in order to grow, need to develop depth and breadth. Through self-disclosure two people begin a friendship that may proceed to the level of intimacy or remain on a casual level. For example, Fred and Tom were in the class of '73 at UCLA. They chance to meet on the streets of Westwood. Both are now in their thirties, moving up in their jobs, and happy to see each other.

"Hi, Fred, it's good to see you! What's new?" they bring each other up-to-date on jobs, wives, children and hobbies. Then they part, satisfied with the brief, casual meeting. This kind of friendship does not depend upon continuity of contact or deeper self-disclosure Neither party expects much from this friendship at this time. Neither man expects a lifetime of sharing time and personal confidences.

Most people will experience numerous friendships. At times they will be active and blossoming. At other times the friendships will lie dormant as lives assume varied dimensions and people travel in different directions. Not each person one meets is destined to be the best friend. As you move along on the continuum of your life and as you change and grow, so it may be with your friendships. They also may change and consequently you can antici-pate reaching out to others along life's path, using many social skills to meet and make friends and, in so doing, constantly enrich the quality of your life.

WHAT TO SAY WHEN

A GUIDE TO MORE EFFECTIVE COMMUNICATION

"DO YOU HEAR ME"?

Chapter 4

Rachel Leeds

Esther Wedner

Bernice Bloch

DO YOU HEAR ME?

WHAT TO SAY WHEN . . .

> . . . you want to be heard and nobody's listening. . .

Lu Ann has returned from a joyous event. She and her brothers and sisters have flown into San Francisco to attend a dinner honoring their sister, Norma. The program is most extraordinary as each of the five sisters and brothers speaks to honor their sister in a moving and dramatic fashion.

When Lu Ann returns to Los Angeles, she has dinner with her good friends, Susan and Mark.

Susan: Lu Ann, how was the weekend?

Lu Ann: It was one of the most beautiful moments of my life.

Susan: How wonderful. Tell us about it.

WHAT TO SAY WHEN

Mark: This chicken is awful.   How's yours, Lu Ann?

Stopped in mid-sentence, Lu Ann swallows hard. Sadly, she realizes Mark has not caught the impact of her special moment; he couldn't care less! He has punctured her balloon!

WHAT TO SAY WHEN

When your husband comes home terribly aggravated because the work order he prepared two weeks ago has been lost on someone's desk, do you listen and say: "Calm down, Harry, why raise your blood pressure?" You think you hear him - but do you?

When your son, Ronnie, dejectedly tells you that Sally refuses to see him for the third time, you listen and say: "You're wasting your time, son. She's not good enough for you!" You think you're a good listener, but are you?

When Mike charges into the house and explodes because his secretary spent valuable time gossiping on the phone, you say: "Now, now dear, don't get excited. You've got to shower and shave. We're going out with the Wilsons at 7:00." Mike struggles for composure. You are puzzled by his tight-lipped facial expression. He slams the door. Did you hear Mike?

WHAT TO SAY WHEN

TYPICAL NON-LISTENING RESPONSES

What do Mike, Harry and Ronnie have in common? Each has chosen to share his concern with a trusted family member. Sad to say, each experiences an unsatisfied need to be heard. Though our situations are contemporary, the problem goes back to the biblical time of Abraham. An Old Testament tale is still relevant.

"Ears they have and they hear not . . . ," said Abraham of the idols he so defiantly repudiated. This bold young iconoclast could not put his faith in unseeing, unhearing, unfeeling, inanimate objects. Nor can we relate today to those whom we consider unhearing and unfeeling. We ask ourselves: "How much trust can we put in those who do not hear us?"

When you tell your friend about Mr. Ronson's unreasonable demands at work and she looks at you momentarily before quickly turning back to the TV set, you know she has not listened to you. You're hurt. Her interest does not seem to be with you. You don't think she cares. She pretends interest. We call this response

WHAT TO SAY WHEN

PSEUDO-LISTENING. *SHE HEARS YOU NOT.*

When you begin to tell your cousin about the fun you had in San Francisco and she interrupts your conversation before you've even described your first meal to speak of HER trip to Tennessee, you know she's heard your last word. She's off and running at the mouth. We call this STAGE-HOGGING. *SHE HEARS YOU NOT.*

When you tell your daughter Sharon: "Gee, Marian looks great. She's as slim as ever!", you're sure to get an angry response. She'll probably say: "Mom, you never get off my back because of my weight." She's so defensive about her appearance that she thinks, "There goes Mom again, criticizing me." Sharon could care less about your good feelings about Marian's slim figure. We call this DEFENSIVE LISTENING. *SHE HEARS YOU NOT.*

When Tim and his dad talk briefly while Dad watches TV, we hear another non-listening response. This one is called AMBUSHING.

WHAT TO SAY WHEN

Father: Hi Tim, how was the game?

Tim: I've had it, Dad. I'm going to sit out the rest of the season and just watch. I'm too thin, too short, too uncoordinated to play football.

Father: I knew it! You never stick with anything. You're a loser! You don't try hard enough. Always excuses, excuses, excuses.

Tim: I knew you wouldn't understand.

Tim comes home feeling crushed and dejected. He wants his father to tune into what he is feeling and to accept it without judgment. His father is so involved in projecting his own ambitions on Tim that *HE HEARS HIM NOT.*

We can see from these examples that the listener who interrupts defensively, insensitively or hoggishly turns off the speaker.

WHAT TO SAY WHEN

TYPICAL HELPING RESPONSES

Often you are called upon to listen to a
friend who is in the throes of some trauma.
Because you want to help, you listen intently
and you may do any of the following: give
advice, analyze, question, deny feelings, or
be sympathetic.   Sometimes your well-
intentioned responses are not helpful at all.
Listen in on some typical responses:

ADVISING

Two friends discuss a problem.

Edna:	I'm really frustrated. Last night I sat for three hours at the City Council meeting, waiting to speak against the new housing proposal and I didn't get to talk.
Nancy:	You should write a letter. Someone'll read it.

That's the end of that particular
conversation.   Nancy's response to her
troubled friend was to give advice. In so
doing, she implied that Edna's strong
feelings were inappropriate. Edna might
say: *"SHE HEARS ME NOT!"*

WHAT TO SAY WHEN

Sometimes, we respond to a friend by <u>asking questions.</u>

ASKING QUESTIONS

Edna: I'm really furious. Last night I sat for three hours at the City Council meeting waiting to speak against the new housing proposal, and I didn't get to talk.

Nancy: Why didn't you sit in the front row?

OR

Edna: I'm really frustrated. Last night I sat for three hours at the meeting, waiting . . .

Nancy: Do you think they ignored you because you're a woman?

Here again, Nancy's <u>questions</u> ignore Edna's distress. Moreover, they direct Edna's response to where Nancy wants to take the conversation. Questions often detract or distract! Because Nancy does not tune into her friend's feelings, Edna might say, *"SHE HEARS ME NOT."*

WHAT TO SAY WHEN

Sometimes we tend to <u>analyze</u> when we respond.

Edna: I'm really frustrated. Last night I
              . . .

Nancy: Maybe the chairman called upon
              people he knew personally.

OR

Edna: I'm really frustrated. Last night I
              . . .

Nancy: Oh. You want to have a say on
              the decision.

When the friend responds analytically, what happens? Nancy implies that anyone could understand the dynamics of the political situation. She also infers that her friend used poor judgment and expects too much. Again, she has lost sight of Edna's need for understanding her feelings.

Comments that analyze ignore feelings. Moreover, the analysis may be incorrect. Even if you're lucky enough to be on target,

WHAT TO SAY WHEN

your partner usually needs time to work through her own plateau of self-awareness. Edna again feels betrayed. *"SHE HEARS ME NOT."*

And then again we often <u>deny feelings</u> when we respond to an agitated friend.

DENYING FEELINGS

Edna: I'm really frustrated. Last night I . . .

Nancy: I don't know what you're getting so excited about. Your turn will come at the next meeting. Besides, you'll have more time to prepare your message.

OR

Edna: I'm really frustrated. Last night I . . .

Nancy: You're always complaining. I haven't heard you say anything good about the City council yet.

Once more, Nancy denies Edna's exasperation by telling her she should not feel that way! Nancy tells Edna that she is over-reacting.

By not permitting the venting of a strong emotion, we cut off further communication. We say, in effect, "You don't have a right to that feeling." Denying Edna's feelings means that Nancy does not have to deal with them. For sure, Edna feels, "*SHE HEARS ME NOT.*"

Another thing we do to excess, oddly enough, is to <u>make excuses</u> for other people's behavior. We do this even when we don't have a stake in the outcome of the problem or know the person we're defending.

MAKING EXCUSES FOR OTHERS

Edna: I'm really frustrated. Last night I . . .

Nancy: I've known the chairman, Mr. Stannis, for years. He likes to take his time and give each speaker his full attention.

OR

WHAT TO SAY WHEN

Edna: I'm really frustrated. Last night I . . .

Nancy: The City council must consider the consequences of our growth. Try to understand that.

Nancy does not hear Edna's grievance. She's too busy apologizing for the City council.

When we make excuses for others, not only are we discounting the speaker's feelings and observations, we are also giving priority to the "other." It must seem a betrayal of trust and certainly the speaker questions your concerns and in frustration claims, *"SHE HEARS ME NOT."*

WHAT WOULD YOU SAY?

Now that we have described the dynamics of typical listening responses, you may find it interesting and helpful to chart your own responses. Make two choices to each situation: your typical responses (T) and your new preferred responses (P).

We believe that now you will begin to see why you made the changes.

WHAT TO SAY WHEN

EXAMPLE:

Gene: "Boy, am I beat! My no-good pal Harry didn't get the software package ready on time. He took off on a vacation while I did all the work. We may lose the Melton account!"

_____	1.	Don't get so steamed. It's not worth raising your blood pressure.
T	2.	I'm sure Harry did the best he could.
_____	3.	What did you say to him: Did you ask him what happened?
P	4.	You're really disappointed. You've lost the deal.

Consider the following dialogues. How would you respond typically (T)? What would be the preferred feedback (P)? Mark your choices.

WHAT TO SAY WHEN

TRY THE FOLLOWING

A. Susan: "When I left home this morning this house was clean. My God, what happened? Now it's a shambles. I'll have to clean it up all over again. You and the kids just don't care!"

_____ 1. You had a hard day today. And you probably have a headache. You're taking it out on us.

_____ 2. You're always finding fault, Mrs. Perfect. We can never relax when you're around.

_____ 3. Didn't the conference go well?

_____ 4. Sounds like you're hurt, Susan. You wanted to see the house nice and tidy after your long, hard day.

B. When your daughter comes home from the class play tryouts and exclaims, "Mom, I made it. I got the lead! There were five other girls in

WHAT TO SAY WHEN

the final readings, and Doctor Jones chose me. Isn't that terrific?"

_____ 1. Sally, you're thrilled. You have the lead in the class play. Isn't that exciting?

_____ 2. Calm down, it looks like you're ready to burst.

_____ 3. You got the lead. That's a big responsibility. How are you going to rehearse and get your homework done?

_____ 4. Sally, you'd better make a study schedule so you can get your work done. When do rehearsals start?

C. "Maria, I know you're David's mother, but I'm plenty worried about his health. He's had a cold for three weeks now. It might go into his ears. I'm afraid he's not dressed warmly enough when he goes out to play."

WHAT TO SAY WHEN

_____ 1. Don't worry about him, Mom. The doctor says three-year-olds get lots of colds.

_____ 2. Mom, you're really concerned about the baby's health. You're afraid he might get an ear infection.

_____ 3. Mom, you're such a worry wart!

_____ 4. Mom, you said it right. I certainly am David's mother and I do know how to take care of my child, thank you!

D. Jerry: "This office shakeup is really giving me problems. We're going to have fewer people to do more work. They asked me to do Sandy's work and mine, too. That's really going too far. I'm already overloaded. I'd need a 52-hour day to get everything done."

_____ 1. I sure feel for you, Jerry. That's a touchy situation.

WHAT TO SAY WHEN

_____ 2.   Why don't you go in to see
            your boss right away? Take
            care of it now. Don't wait.

_____ 3.   I think you're making a
            mountain out of a mole hill.
            It's not going to be so bad.
            Let's give it a chance!

_____ 4.   You're feeling pressure
            already. And you're dreading
            what the future holds.

E.   Boss: "I don't know what we'll do
      about Bill Samson. He's so creative
      and he's got lots of enthusiasm. And
      when you talk to him you get a sense
      of his salesmanship. But his reports
      are always late. His accounts are
      sometimes left up in the air. We
      can't count on Bill 100%.

_____ 1.   Well, nobody's perfect. We
            can't expect a top-notch
            salesman to be a good book-
            keeper.

_____ 2.   Bill's had an awful lot of
            personal problems lately. Did

WHAT TO SAY WHEN

you know his wife was in the hospital?

_____ 3. You have mixed feelings about Bill. You admire him but at the same time you're disappointed. He's a great salesman but he doesn't always deliver.

_____ 4. I never thought he'd make it. I told you so.

After examining your listening responses, have you noticed a tendency to respond in the same way to each situation? Do you question, or advise, or analyze? Or have you caught on to active listening? For each dialogue, an active listening response reflected back to the speaker the gist of his message and/or the feeling implied.

CHECK YOUR RESPONSES

For Gene, #4: "You're really disappointed, you've lost the deal." Reflects his own feelings and summarizes his situation.

WHAT TO SAY WHEN

For Susan, #4: "Sounds like you're hurt, Susan. You wanted to see the house nice and tidy after your long, hard, day." Reflects her feelings and paraphrases her message.

For Sally, #1. "Sally, you're thrilled. You have the lead in the class play. Isn't that exciting!" Paraphrases her message and reflects her feelings.

In grandma's case, it's #2; and for Jerry, it"s #4; and in the personnel director's case, #3 is a reflective message.

In summary, it appears that your normal, routine responses as listeners impede rather than facilitate helpful exchange. When husbands tell their wives about exasperating problems in their jobs, do they really want advice? Sometimes, but rarely. When wives

WHAT TO SAY WHEN

tell their husbands how they feel about mother's nagging or daughter's latest emotional outburst, do they want a logical, practical solution? Not usually.

When you are brimming over with dismay and anxiety or flowing with good feelings, you want your partner to listen empathetically, without advice, without analysis, without discounting. You need your partners to set aside their values, their expectations, and their personal agendas long enough to step into your shoes. How? By active listening!

WHAT TO SAY WHEN

A GUIDE TO MORE EFFECTIVE COMMUNICATION

"CAN YOU TUNE IN"?

Chapter 5

Rachel Leeds

Esther Wedner

Bernice Bloch

CAN YOU TUNE IN?

WHAT TO SAY WHEN . . .

    . . . you need to hear the feelings of the people in your life . . .

Phoebe and her colleague have just finished another day of teaching.

Phoebe:	I don't know where my grade book is for the geography class. I'm going out of my mind. I tell myself that I won't take those record books home, but I have to do some of the papers on the weekend. Where in the world could I have put them?
Listener:	YOU SEEM FRANTIC, PHOEBE.
Phoebe:	Whew, I think I'm getting "old-timer's" disease!
Listener:	YOU'RE REALLY WORRIED ABOUT AGING!

Phoebe: If I don't simplify my life, I'm in deep trouble.

The listener has tuned in: Phoebe feels understood and accepted.

The greatest gift you can present to someone is your listening presence: to be attentive, to tune into their feelings and to understand their needs. You know you're not alone in this world when someone takes the time to really hear you.

Simply listening is not so simple. What listening does for another can be the best you can do for that person at their moment of need. Your attention can serve as a catalyst to help the person make a decision or calm a fear. Contrary to the popular practice of offering help, advising, or analyzing the speaker's problem, active listening seeks to assure the speaker that you value and understand him. You have faith that he can resolve his own conflict. Listening can assure the speaker that he is valued and understood.

This kind of tuning in requires ears to hear the words, eye to observe the body language, and understanding to let your partners know that you hear what they say and discern how they feel. We call this kind of listening involvement AC-TIVE LISTENING.

There are two basic kinds of feedback which the active listener provides the speaker. First, your understanding of the message is conveyed by *paraphrasing*. You use your own words to sum-marize the speaker's comments. Second, your empathy with the speaker is expressed as you reflect the feelings you sense.

These conversations illustrate the listener's use of *paraphrasing* to reflect an understanding of the message content.

Danny: Grandma, I miss you. I wish I was back in California. I had fun at your house. There were so many kids to play with. The kids here are mean. They chase me and call me names.

WHAT TO SAY WHEN

Listener:	I CAN SEE WHY YOU MISS YOUR CALIFORNIA FRIENDS. SOUNDS LIKE THE KIDS AT HOME ARE TRYING TO BULLY YOU, DANNY.

* * *

Nurse:	I ran my feet off for Mrs. Ramsay. No sooner did I answer her light when she put it on again.
Listener:	SHE REALLY WORE YOU OUT WITH ALL THAT RUNNING.

* * *

Michelle:	Gerry, I have great news!
Listener:	YOU DO? WHAT HAPPENED?
Michelle:	I got elected to the literary honors society at school and I get to take a class at UCLA next semester while I'm a senior at high school. Now I'm sure I'll get

WHAT TO SAY WHEN

into UCLA. Wow! Everything's going
my way!

Listener: SOUNDS LIKE YOU'RE REALLY
FLYING, HONEY. YOU GOT WHAT
YOU WERE GOING FOR.

When you *paraphrase*, you feed back your understanding of the message. Not like a parrot, not
like a tape recorder. You reflect back the content so that the speakers have a chance to hear
themselves and you have checked your understanding of their messages.

REFLECTING FEELINGS is the second part of
the process. You let the speakers know that you
have tuned into their implied feelings - the heart
of the message. Sometimes that seems even
more appropriate and critical than to reflect back
the content.

The following dialogues illustrate the reflection of the
speaker's feelings:

Joseph: The insurance company will cancel my
               car insurance if I don't get $160 to them
               by tomorrow. God, it seems like I work
               just to keep up with old debts and more
               bills.

Listener: YOU'RE WORRIED AND DISCOUR-
               AGED, AREN'T YOU?

Joseph: It really gets to me. But, I'm better off
               than I was. It just takes so long to pay
               everything off. I'll be alright.

                         * * *

Evelyn: We forgot to tape record the poem I
               read at mother's party the other night.
               So I asked her if she wanted me to tape
               it now. After all, it was a summary of
               some of her own personal history, and
               she said, "NO!"

WHAT TO SAY WHEN

Listener: YOU MUST HAVE BEEN SO HURT, EVELYN . . . AFTER ALL THAT CREATIVE EFFORT!

Evelyn: Yes, but I should know my mother by now. All she seemed to care about were the food and the flowers. She doesn't care about what I did to make her birthday special.

Listener: IT REALLY BOTHERS YOU, EVELYN, THAT SHE COULD CARE LESS ABOUT YOUR HELP.

* * *

Jessica: I'm at a serious crossroads in my life and I can't seem to make a decision. I used to make up my mind quickly and easily. But now that I'm in my 60's, I feel very insecure. Of course when Rick was alive we talked things over. Since his death, I don't know what to do about staying in this house, investing my mon-

WHAT TO SAY WHEN

	ey, even how to take care of the car. I feel like crying all the time.
Linda:	IT SOUNDS TO ME AS IF YOU FEEL ANXIOUS ABOUT YOUR DECISIONS SINCE YOUR HUSBAND DIED. IT'S REALLY SCARY TO MAKE MAJOR DECISIONS ALONE.
Jessica:	Yes, that's true. I thought I'd be able to handle things better as time goes by. But instead, I seem to need lots of reassurance. Should I do this? Should I do that? Everyone goes through this, I've heard, but what a problem it is.

When you begin using a new way of listening, you may experience some difficulty in finding just the right words to use in reflecting your own responses. That's only natural. To give you an opportunity to practice *reflective listening* responses, study the next four examples. Then practice this skill yourself.   As your practice increases, you are going to become more at ease in giving *reflective listening* responses.

Again, try not to echo or parrot the exact words used by the speaker. You can begin your statement or question by saying such phrases as: "Sounds like," "It seems to me . . ." "I wonder if . . ." "Are you feeling . . ." Remember, you are asked to listen and *reflect the substance of the message* and the speaker's *feelings*.

Ellie: I don't know how much longer I should wait for Bill to fix the roof on our patio. He said he'd come last week and I haven't heard from him yet.

Dan: BILL HASN'T SHOWN UP AND YOU DON'T KNOW WHAT TO DO ABOUT THE PATIO.

Ellie: Yes, and I'm getting fed up. Does he expect me to wait for him forever? Susan's wedding is only

WHAT TO SAY WHEN

a month away and we'll never have the patio ready on time!

Dan: SOUNDS LIKE YOU'RE FEELING FRANTIC AT THIS STAGE.

* * *

John: Al, I'm having lots of trouble getting along with Mr. Thompson. This computer program is Greek to me and to most of the other students too. Thompson expects us to understand how to do it alone.

Al: YOU FEEL CONFUSED AND ANGRY BE-CAUSE YOUR TEACHER IS NOT HELPING YOU UNDERSTAND THE WORK.

John: Yeah, that's it exactly. And you know what else? He always talks down to us. I'm afraid to ask a question because I'm sure he'll make fun of me! That's no way to teach. He acts like some kind of hotshot. He really makes me mad!

WHAT TO SAY WHEN

Al: YOU'RE DISGUSTED WITH HIS ARRO-GANCE.

John: Yeah. I think we have to organize a group to talk to the man. I'm going to talk to Andy and Fred.

* * *

Ann: My mother is horrified about my pregnancy. She thinks I'm selfish to want to keep the baby because I'm not married.

Josie: YOU'RE REALLY HURTING BECAUSE YOUR MOM IS DEAD SET AGAINST YOUR KEEPING THE BABY.

Ann: Yes, you're right. I'm very upset. She's not making it easy for me, that's for sure. Guess I'll have to go through this pregnancy alone. I thought she'd be happy to have a grandchild.

Josie: YOU FEEL REJECTED AT A TIME WHEN YOU NEED YOUR MOTHER. YOU

WHAT TO SAY WHEN

THOUGHT SHE'D BE HAPPY WHEN YOU
DECIDED TO KEEP THE BABY.

Ann: You said it! I'm so disappointed and hurt. I
never dreamed she'd give me so much flack! I'll
have to go it alone.

* * *

Karen: Listen here, Mr. Lawyer. I want to renegotiate
our marriage contract. I DO NOT want to go to
your mother's every Sunday for dinner. I DO
NOT want to go bowling every Wednesday
night. I'm fed up with the same old routine.

Bob: SOUNDS LIKE YOU'RE FED UP WITH THE
WAY THINGS ARE.

Karen: Yes, I am. I don't feel like I count. I always
cater to your needs.

Bob: I DIDN'T REALIZE THAT YOU FEEL SO
ANGRY ABOUT OUR WEEKLY ROUTINE.
IF YOU FEEL LEFT OUT OF THE DECI-
SIONS, LET'S TALK ABOUT IT, KAREN.

WHAT TO SAY WHEN

Now practice completing the following examples.

Sam: It really worries me that Mother lives alone. She's pretty self-sufficient at 83, but I still worry. Is she eating okay? Is she lonely? Is she getting out? Is she seeing friends?

Henry: YOU'RE REALLY WORRIED ABOUT MOM.

Sam: Since she doesn't want to live with us - what about a retirement home? She'd get her meals, have a clean room, and other people around. But somehow, that bothers me.

Henry: _____

_____

_____

_____

WHAT TO SAY WHEN

Here are Jeff and David, two colleagues, discussing a problem.

Jeff: I don't know whether to leave Maria alone right now. She's really depressed since she miscarried. We both wanted this baby so much. But my agent just called. There's a spot in the arthritis telethon in Vegas next week.

Dave: YOU WANT TO GO TO VEGAS BUT YOU'RE WORRIED ABOUT LEAVING MARIA.

Jeff: Yes, I'd like the opportunity. This gig could be the break I've been waiting for. I really want to do a stand-up role in a Vegas lounge show. That could happen if they like me in the telethon. Why can't life be simple?

Dave: _____

_____

_____

* * *

Tom: I'm so exhausted, Suzy. Working two jobs is sure tough. When I get home the kids are in bed and I'm too tired to do anything but hit the sack myself!

Suzy: THE WORK ROUTINE IS GETTING TO BE TOO MUCH FOR YOU. IS THAT WHAT YOU'RE SAYING?

Tom: That's it, Suzy. I can't even play with the kids except on the weekends. There's got to be more to life than work, work, work.

Suzy: _____

_____

_____

_____

WHAT TO SAY WHEN

Usually when someone talks to us about a problem, we think we have to solve it. We put out our FIX IT KIT. If Plan A doesn't work, then we suggest Plan B. We have been trained from early childhood to do something. That's why most of us respond with advice.

We are suggesting an alternative listening response that sounds very strange, almost a "do-nothing" imperative. But that's not true, either. What we are proposing are new ways of listening and responding that will strengthen your understanding of your partner. When you paraphrase, you tell the speaker that you understand the message and that you want to hear more. In addition, you let them know that their feelings have been heard without judgment. Paradoxically, as the active listener, you can help the speaker hear *himself* with greater clarity so that he finds the answers he seeks within himself.

Incorporating any new skill takes time and awareness. Active listening may seem unnatural and

WHAT TO SAY WHEN

awkward when first implemented. We suggest that you incorporate the paraphrasing gradually. Become sensitive to unexpressed feelings and reflect these when appropriate.

To summarize, we take the word *reflective* literally: to think or ponder about some idea, problem or event. That's precisely what the listener is called upon to do at this point. No advice. No tsk, tsk, tsk. No amateur psychiatry. Just listening. A difficult task for most of us. In time, however, this kind of *reflective* response offers many rewards at both ends of the conversation.

Just a listening ear,
Free and clear.
I HEAR YOU, PARTNER!

WHAT TO SAY WHEN

A GUIDE TO MORE EFFECTIVE COMMUNICATION

"DO YOU TELL IT LIKE IT IS"?

Chapter 6

Rachel Leeds

Esther Wedner

Bernice Bloch

DO YOU TELL IT LIKE IT IS?

What to Say When . . .

. . . your insides are simmering from the heat of dissatisfaction and you want to tell it like it is . . .

In the scenario below Rudy and Sybil are in the thick of a confrontation. Listen in:

Sybil: Rudy, help me carry in a package from the car.

Rudy: A package! Something new? What did you buy now?

Sybil: You'll see, it's a painting I got at the auction.

Rudy: A painting? We just agreed to make a joint decision on big buys! How could you go back on your promise?

Sybil: Rudy, don't treat me like a child. This painting is an investment. Can't you trust me to make a decision alone when a special deal comes up?

Rudy: *Trust you?* You can't be trusted at all! You're a shopaholic! Buy, buy buy; that's all you do. You need a psychiatrist.

Sybil: I can't believe this. You're such a fool. I've had it! Get your own dinner! I'm going to the gym!

WHAT TO SAY WHEN

Sybil and Rudy are reacting to their problem in a destructive manner.

Now come along with us while we explain a technique we call the BEF. It's a message that allows you to be honest without being hurtful, assertive without being arrogant, to say "I" instead of "YOU." Delivering a BEF, using the best descriptive language for each of its parts, enables you to change from arguing to presenting, from timidity to telling it like it is, from confusion to clarity.

Have you ever wondered what causes many relationships to flounder and fail? Is it sex? Religion? Money? Is it control? Perhaps these are contributing factors. But we believe the primary reason is failure to communicate effectively.

Let's see how differences about the spending of money are communicated, since almost everyone argues about money . . . getting it, spending it, saving it, and not having it.

"When it comes to spending money, Henry, you don't."

"Cindy, you'd spend every dime I make on clothes if I'd let you."

"Mom, why do I have to pay all your bills now that dad's passed away? You must know how to write a check!"

Clearly, these remarks attack: putting the receiver on the defensive. They are blaming messages.

How do you think Henry feels?
What will Cindy say to her husband's accusation?
Will Mom feel hurt by her son's outburst?

We think that Henry would get hot under the collar, that Cindy would grit her teeth and become defensive, and that Mom would burst into tears.

1.   Henry's wife is *critical:* *"You're* tight."

2.   Cindy's husband *blames:*   "Cindy, *you're* bankrupting us."

3.   Mom's son *complains: "You* pressure me."

"YOU" messages make us bristle. They attack and put us down. Nobody likes to be discounted. The complainer has a long-standing, deep-seated grievance that has finally surfaced. You may wonder why these combatants have not talked? Well, they have. But their interaction, their "YOU" messages, have exacerbated the conflict.

WHAT TO SAY WHEN

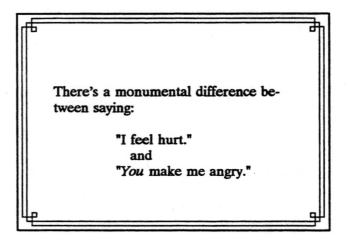

There's a monumental difference between saying:

"I feel hurt."
and
"You make me angry."

Instead of a "YOU" attack, make a disclosing "I"
message, which tells:

What I see
What I experience
What I feel
What I want

With an "I" message, I can reveal my perceptions
and my problem. My problem? It is *my* problem
because "I" have to cope with my partner's behavior.

Henry doesn't have a problem saving a buck.

Cindy doesn't have a problem buying the latest fashions.

Mom doesn't have a problem asking her son to get the bills paid.

Use the "I" message. It avoids the adversarial role. It builds bridges across your differences.

We call the "I" message a "BEF." Because we often refer to a complaint as a BEF.

To explain your concern concisely and constructively, follow this formula:

"B"_____   Describe the behavior

"E"_____   Describe the effect or consequence of that behavior

"F"_____   Describe the feeling

"B" _____ Describes Behavior

When talking about "behavior," address the specific action that concerns you.

> Henry's thriftiness
> Cindy's extravagance
> Mom's helplessness.

Focus on the action the same way you look at a slide through a viewer. Freeze this particular situation since it's the issue. Give the other person that information.

Do not be distracted by your partner's anxiety. This liberates you from personalizing the conflict. You can stand back and present the BEF calmly. Stay in control.

> You do not blame.
> You do not criticize.
> You scrutinize!

Now, let's look back at the frames that caught the action involving Henry, Cindy, and Mom and describe the offending BEHAVIOR.

Henry's wife:	"Henry, when I tell you we need a new refrigerator because this one doesn't keep cold, my comments are ignored."
Cindy's husband:	"Cindy, according to our budget, the car payment has top priority. But a third of my paycheck went for your new clothes.
The son:	"Mom, the first of every month I have to come over to pay your bills because you worry and stew about it."

This part of the message (the "B" in BEFS) has specifically described BEHAVIOR.

WHAT TO SAY WHEN

"E"_____Describe Effects

The "E" part of the message describes the EF-FECTS, the tangible, concrete consequences of the partner's behavior.

Henry's wife:

"Henry, when I tell you we need a new refrigerator because this one doesn't keep cool, my comments are ignored. YESTERDAY, I THREW OUT THE ROAST. IT DOESN'T KEEP THE MEAT FRESH.

Cindy's husband:

"Cindy, according to our budget, the car payment has top priority. But almost a third of our money went for clothes. NOW I CAN'T MAKE THE CAR PAYMENT!"

The son:

"Mom, every first of the month I have to come over and pay your bills because you worry and fret. I HAVE TO LEAVE WORK EARLY AND RETURN TO THE OFFICE LATE TO CATCH UP ON MY OWN WORK."

Why describe the *effect* of the behavior? Because most people are so absorbed in their own agendas that they frequently are unaware of the consequences of their behavior. No one has a way of accurately reading another's head talk. To prevent confusion and misunderstanding, the aggrieved person needs to tell the "other" what happens as a result of their behavior. For example, you might say:

> "I can't concentrate and I get a headache when the stereo is so loud. I have to study for my chem test."

The listener can identify with the irritation caused by the volume of the stereo. On the other hand, when you describe a less tangible effect such as:

> "That rock sound drives me up the wall!"

the ambiguity of your statement might prompt a comment such as:

> "You get upset over every little thing."

WHAT TO SAY WHEN

So far, the two elements . . . Behavior and Effect
. . . have been discussed. Recalling the viewer
analogy, the **behavior** has been held up to the
light and its *effect* revealed.

"F" _____ Describe FEELINGS

Now, use the "F" element in the formula: a description of the emotion experienced through the troubling event. Tell what you FEEL.

> "Henry, every time I tell you we need a new refrigerator because this one doesn't keep cold, my comments are ignored. Yesterday, I threw out the roast because it wasn't fresh. I FEEL RESENT-FUL AND ALTOGETHER DIS-COURAGED."

> " Cindy, according to our budget, the car payment has top priority, but almost a third of this month's money went for clothes. Now I can't make the car payment. I FEEL PRESSURED AND BE-TRAYED."

> "Mom, every month I have to come over on the first to pay your bills

because you worry and fret. I have to leave work early and return to the office late to catch up on my own work. I'M FEELING FRUS-TRATED."

Notice that these messages reflect the injured person's view and pain. At no time is there threat, attack or bad-mouthing of the other person. Rather, *there is a constructive attempt to make clear to the listener the speaker's honest response to a troubling situation.* The temptation is great to load up the argument with all kinds of complaints. Don't do it!

The third element of the BEF - "F" - *feeling* - expresses the emotions which inevitably accompany a troubling experience.

To further clarify the concept of the BEF, we present a chart followed by simple situations. Because it may be difficult to distinguish between the EFFECT and FEELINGS, we have examples to help you recognize the <u>difference</u> between the two reactions. The section that follows gives you a chance to identify the different elements of the BEF.

WHAT TO SAY WHEN

Observable Behavior	Effects	Feeling
Loud stereo	I can't sleep	angry furious frustrated
Check bounces	I pay a penalty	angry frustrated trapped
Paycheck is late	I can't pay bills	angry furious hurt
Late dinner guests	Dinner is spoiled	resentful
Flirting with my husband	I cancel my friendship	hurt betrayed angry
Calling my opinions "immature"	I don't share my thoughts with you	put-down, dimin-ished
When interrupted	I lose my train of thought	frustrated disturbed

"S" _____ Specify what you want.

You might want to stop with your expression of the three parts of the BEF. However, sometimes that isn't enough. Add one more element to the message. "S" . . . BEFS! "S" symbolizes the word "Specify." To specify is to tell what change is desired.

You need to specify what you want! Unless you say what you want, your partner may come up with a different and unacceptable change. Henry would get the old refrigerator fixed. Cindy might cry and say, "You don't love me," and Mom might sulk and exclaim, "I'll never ask you to do anything for me again."

What does Henry's wife want? Tired of making do with an old refrigerator, she says, loud and clear: "I want to buy a new refrigerator."

What does Cindy's husband want? He isn't mean and he isn't into control. He wants Cindy to develop with him the priorities they should share in spending money. He tells her: "I want you to work with me in setting up a budget."

WHAT TO SAY WHEN

What does the dutiful son want? Pressured and resentful, he finally speaks up calmly and resolutely: "Mom, I want you to learn how to take care of your bills. I'll show you how to do it. Then we can spend time together relaxing and doing something we both enjoy."

As we reflect upon each problem situation, you may ask: Was the concern in each illustration really about money? We don't think so. The problem arose because each pair of disgruntled people had been guilty of several "misdemeanors":

1. They allowed the offending behaviors to continue for a long time.

2. They failed to use "I" messages and so did not take the responsibility for having their perceptions and feelings about the troubling situations.

3. They failed to focus on one specific behavior.

4. They did not express the effects of the undesirable actions.

WHAT TO SAY WHEN

5.   They avoided expressing their feelings.

6.   They did not specify desirable changes.

Let's look at the interactions which might have occurred if the aggrieved had informed their partners with a BEF message.

Remember Alice has been frustrated by Henry's unwillingness to purchase a new refrigerator.

Alice: "Henry, I'm glad to see you so relaxed this evening; but I want to talk about something that's been bothering me for some time."

Henry: "Okay, Alice, What's on your mind?"

Alice: "Every time I tell you we need a new refrigerator because this one doesn't stay cold, you ignore me. Yesterday I threw out a roast. I feel frustrated and plain discouraged."

Henry: "Well, hell, Alice. I didn't think the old box was that bad! But if it's gotten to the point where the food spoils, I think 'old reliable' may not be so reliable any more. Do you think we could fix it again?"

Alice: "We did have the repairman just three months ago and he told us then it might need a new motor soon. They are expensive, Henry, and besides, I don't think this size is adequate any more."

Henry: "Well, let's look at our budget and see what we can afford. You know I'm really attached to that box. We've had it since we were married."

Alice: "Oh, Henry. You're such a sentimental fool. You're not getting rid of me, only a worn-out refrigerator!"

When Cindy's husband, Tom, uses the BEF, he probably can expect, at the very least, a receptive ear instead of a turned-off pout.

Tom: "Cindy, we just got this bill. We have to talk!"

Cindy: "Okay, Tom. Dinner's not quite ready. What's up?"

WHAT TO SAY WHEN

Tom: "According to our budget, the car payment has top priority. Now I get this bill showing $300 for a coat! I can't make the car payment! I'm feeling pressured and downright depressed."

Cindy: "Gee, I needed the coat. I guess I didn't realize I was being so extravagant. I get carried away by sales."

Tom: "Cindy, I want you to sit down and work on this budget with me."

Cindy: "I guess you're right! If we can work out a clothing allowance, that might help me to stay within limits. I'm sorry, honey."

Remember the son who feels hassled by his mother's pressure to pay her bills the first of the month? The following dialogue illustrates an improved interaction.

Son: "Hi, Mom. It's Tuesday, the first of the month. Here I am again."

Mother: "Hi, dear. It's good to see you, but you look upset. Is something wrong?"

Son: "Mom, I _am_ upset and tired, too. I didn't know how to say this before but now is as good a time as ever. I feel pressured each time I come over to pay your bills."

Mother: "Why? What do you mean? You always did it for me and never complained before."

Son: "I know, Mom. What bothers me is that you're anxious about the first of the month payments when I'm busiest at my office. When I'm finished here, I have to go back to finish my work. It makes a long day for me."

Mother: "I don't know what to say. What can I do?"

Son: "Well, for openers, you can write out the checks you know are correct: your utilities and the house payments. Then I'll look at anything you have questions about. How does that sound? And I'm still going to come over and see you at a more convenient time."

Mother: "That sounds fine. I can do that, I'm sure."

Son: "That would give us more time to visit together. That would be great."

WHAT TO SAY WHEN

Mother: "I'm so glad you told me. I want our time together to be pleasant."

Son: "Thanks, Mom. That makes me feel good."

Sometimes in a conflict situation it's unnecessary to use all the elements of the BEF. Often just describing what bothers you (the Behavior) and expressing your feelings will start the dialogue. For some, especially men who are unaccustomed to expressing feelings, and often are intimidated by them; describing the behavior and its *effect* may be all that's needed. For example:

"When you turn away while I'm talking to you, I feel frustrated." (Feeling)

or

"When you turn while I'm talking to you, I drop the subject." (Effect)

"I lent you $100 six months ago and you were going to repay me in one month and now I can't pay my gas bill." (Effect)

As you can see from these examples, it does not take lengthy explanations to open the channels of communication. Of course, temper, tone of voice and timing all enter into this delicate area of communication. When BEFS are expressed calmly and with polite language, we are more likely to be heard and get what we want than when we nag and attack.

It may take several reruns of your BEFS to effect change. Remember that you may be addressing an old grievance or habitual patterns. Specifying what you want does not automatically mean you achieve the desired change.

Bear in mind that although you have clearly, politely, and honestly expressed your position, it may be difficult for your partners to accede to your request. They may need much more time to assimilate the information, weigh its merits, and decide what action to take.

For example, Henry may not have the money to buy a new refrigerator at this time. Cindy may need convincing that by cutting down on clothes expenses and getting the car payments made without a hassle, she will profit. Mom may feel helpless and abandoned when her son demands that she learn how to write her own checks and take care of her own business matters.

Working together, you can deal with the particular situation and hopefully resolve the conflict to your mutual satisfaction. Furthermore, your sharing of your own perceptions sets a new pattern for dealing with differences and becomes a model for honest interaction. You teach others how to respond by your communication behavior.

Usually the behaviors that distress us are part of the nitty gritty of daily living. It's not likely that they'll make the evening news! A mother finally tells her son *calmly* that she wants him to contribute to the household expenses. Finally, Grandma gathers courage to say: "I like to be asked my opinion, too. I'm part of the family."

Nobody can read your mind. You can tell it like it is! That means tell what you see, what happens as a result, what you feel and what you want. You clear the air because you have made yourself "perfectly clear" - with your "BEF"!

PRACTICE THE BEF

Now, see if you can identify the different elements of the BEFS: Elaine and Dorothy, who were best friends, graduated from high school ten years ago. They have not kept in close touch. Elaine feels hurt. She considers the BEF and decides to tell Dorothy how she feels. Let's listen in on their phone conversation.

Dorothy: "Hello."

Elaine: "Hi, Dorothy. I thought I'd give you a call before our class reunion."

Dorothy: "How nice. What's doing?"

Elaine: "To tell you the truth - I've finally gathered the courage to tell you something that's been bothering me for a long time."

Dorothy: "What's wrong?"

Elaine: "Well - it seems like I'm the one who always calls you. I think maybe I'm pushing our friendship."

WHAT TO SAY WHEN

Dorothy: "You're saying that because I don't call you I don't value our friendship?"

Elaine: "Yes, that's it! You said it better than I."

Dorothy: "Oh, Elaine, I may not call you, but our friendship does mean a lot to me and I'm sorry you feel unsure about that. I'm on the phone so much at the office that I never pick it up at home. I rarely call anybody at night."

Elaine: "I'm on the phone all day too. I can't sell houses without making lots of phone calls.

Dorothy: "Gee, that's true."

Elaine: "If you pick up the phone and call me sometime, I would feel a lot better."

Dorothy: "Sure. Thanks for being so honest. You're a good friend., I'm looking forward to seeing you at the reunion. And I'll call you up to set the time. Okay?"

Elaine: "Okay, Dorothy. Bye now."

Now look back at the message and identify "B" - the BEHAVIOR; "E" - the EFFECTS; "F" - the FEELINGS; and "S" - SPECIFY the change wanted.

What is the "B" that Elaine describes?

_____

_____

_____

_____

What effect does the behavior have on Elaine?

_____

_____

_____

What feeling does Elaine have?

_____

_____

_____

What does Elaine want?

_____

_____

_____

_____

_____

In case you want to check out the correctness of your response about Dorothy and Elaine, some brief answers are provided.

- Elaine says that Dorothy never calls her. (BEHAVIOR)

- Elaine wonders if the friendship is one-sided. (EFFECT)

- Elaine feels insecure; distrustful. (FEELING)

- Elaine wants Dorothy to call her sometimes. (SPECIFY change)

The dialogues that follow deal with a variety of problems in different settings. While reading

them, try to visualize the characters and imagine
how they feel. Are their methods of dealing with
problems similar to yours?

Joe and Matt work together in a big corporation.
They like each other a lot. But there's a problem
here, too. Joe, the supervisor, is a perfectionist.
Matt is a little more relaxed. Their problem
concerns defensive behavior.

> **Joe:** "Matt, did you get the specifications laid
> out for the Saxe job?"
>
> **Matt:** "Well, I just got a look at them yesterday,
> so . . . "
>
> **Joe:** "Just tell me 'yes' or 'no'!"
>
> **Matt:** "You know, Joe, when you talk to me in
> that tone of voice, I get defensive. I feel
> like a kid whose dad tells him he didn't do
> the chores. I feel embarrassed, yes, and
> angry, too."
>
> **Joe:** "What are you talking about? I just want
> to know how much time to allocate on the
> Saxe job for next week."
>
> **Matt:** "Well, Joe, maybe you could change your
> tone of voice. Or you could tell me why
> you want to know. This "tell me 'yes' or
> 'no' business I find hard to handle.

Joe: "I didn't realize you felt that way. I must have sounded very harsh. Sorry; I'm glad you told me.

What is the "B" in Matt's BEF?

_____

_____

_____

_____

What is the "E" in Matt's BEF?

_____

_____

_____

How does Matt feel?

_____

_____

_____

_____

WHAT TO SAY WHEN

Leonard and his wife, Dolores, face some serious health problems. She's handicapped and walks with crutches. Leonard bends over backwards to assist Dolores with the household chores. But sometimes his helpfulness is a problem, too.

Dolores: "Look, Len, I know you want to help me clean up the kitchen. But when you don't let me empty the dishwasher when I feel up to it, I feel like a helpless baby."

Len: "I'm only trying to help. It's so hard for you to take care of the house."

Dolores: "I know you mean well, honey, but when you stop me, I lose my independence."

Len: "I don't understand. So what should I do?"

Dolores: "Trust me to use good judgment about what I can do. I'll tell you when I need help. But if I want to do something that isn't going to hurt me, I will. Understand?"

Len: "Gotcha."

WHAT TO SAY WHEN

What is the "B" in Dolores' BEF?

_____

_____

_____

_____

What EFFECTS does the behavior have on her?

_____

_____

_____

What FEELINGS does she express?

_____

_____

_____

_____

What does she WANT from Len?

_____

_____

_____

_____

WHAT TO SAY WHEN

ASK YOURSELF

#1.   When your husband asks why you spent $50 on books, do you justify your expenditure? Do you feel resentful for having to explain?

#2.   When your wife says she'd like to go to a fish restaurant tonight and you want a nice juicy hamburger, do you wind up eating fish? What do you say? How do you feel?

#3.   When your son manipulates you into buying yet another Atari game and you already have spent next week's food allotment, what do you say? How do you feel?

#4.   When your best friend agrees to meet you for lunch at 12:30 and shows up at 2:00, what do you say? How do you feel?

#5.   When your boss has promised you a job review in two months but six months have gone by without a talk, what do you say? How do you feel?

#6.   When your neighbor asks you to feed the
        dog for two weeks and stays away for
        four weeks without letting you know,
        what do you say? How do you feel?

To give yourself more practice in the use of
BEFS, you may want to write out scripts which
will describe the disturbing BEHAVIOR, indicate
the EFFECT or consequences, express the
FEELING and SPECIFY the desired change.
For example, you might respond to situation #1
above with:

"When I am asked to explain why I spend $50 on books,
I resent it because I think I'm being treated like a child.
I want you to express your feelings honestly by saying, 'It
bothers me that you buy books now when we're hurting
for money.'"

In summary, the BEF helps us to focus on one
particular problem behavior.

- We clarify our perception of the BE-
  HAVIOR to our partner.

- We describe the EFFECT upon us of
  that BEHAVIOR.

- We disclose our FEELINGS.

- We SPECIFY what change we want to
  see.

WHAT TO SAY WHEN

A GUIDE TO MORE EFFECTIVE COMMUNICATION

"WHAT'S YOUR COMFORT ZONE"?

Chapter 7

Rachel Leeds

Esther Wedner

Bernice Bloch

WHAT'S YOUR COMFORT ZONE?

WHAT TO SAY WHEN . . .

. . . the emotional climate around you is too hot or too cold for comfort.

Your teen-age daughter wants to wear a strapless dress to church. It's summer. She wants to show off her tan. You feel it's inappropriate. You know everyone is going to glare at her as you walk in together. What do you do? What do you say?

Mother: "You look like a little tramp. Nobody goes to church looking like that. If you wear that dress, you're not going with me. I'm not going to have my good name spoiled because my daughter comes to church like that."

Daughter: "I'm not going! If I'm not good enough the way I look, go by yourself!"

WHAT TO SAY WHEN

It looks like the climate surrounding mother and daughter is too hot for comfort!

Just as a plant thrives with suitable temperature, so does communication flower in an appropriate climate. Communication withers in extreme temperatures. Berate someone and you are likely to get a "steamed" response to those fighting words. Ignore someone and you'll get a "chilly" reply of withdrawal. Criticism and indifference are two behaviors which generate hostile climates.

However, supportive messages serve as alternatives to counterproductive patterns of communication. For example, instead of criticism, we can objectively describe what bothers us. Instead of indifference, we can deliver an empathetic message.

Jack Gibb's landmark study on group behavior cited six responses which generate defensiveness and six alternative messages which create a warm, accepting climate. Before we examine each of these, let's hear some typical defensive responses to negative messages.

WHAT TO SAY WHEN

Most of us bristle when we are criticized. Evaluation has been recognized as the single greatest
barrier to communication. Unless we deliberately
ask for critiques of a skill we want to improve,
most of us feel threatened when we think our
appearance or actions displease.

Imagine how upset you may be:

> When your carefully prepared report
> receives the acid comment: "When are
> you going to learn how to spell?"

> When your intelligence is directly assault-
> ed: "That was a stupid thing to do!"

> When your motivation is questioned:
> "You're only interested in what's in it for
> you!"

> When your appearance is considered
> unattractive: "Gad, what happened to
> you? You look like the wrath of God!"

So, why do you worry and brood over these comments? It has to do with how you think about

yourself. In your heart of hearts, you may well picture yourself as

-      **Competent (and he criticized my report!)**

-      **Intelligent (<u>me</u> stupid?)**

-      **Altruistic (I'm selfish?)**

-      **Unattractive (do I look bad?)**

These attributes of your self image are being stripped away by your critics. So you feel threatened and in the rush to defend yourself, you will "fight or take flight."

How do you fight? You can say something nasty to your critic, "You're a fool. I've had it with your nit picking!" Or, "Look who's talking! You never get anything straight."

On the other hand, if you feel hurt and intimidated and don't feel like fighting, you might take flight and say, "What the heck, you win some, you lose some," You withdraw from any interaction with your partner. You bury your resentment. The result is no communication and very little relating.

WHAT TO SAY WHEN

So the hurt person takes flight by not communicating aloud. He may tell himself that his critic never takes his suggestions anyway. "I'm going to keep my mouth shut from now on" or "Mr. Big Shot's running off at the mouth again."

Fight through verbal aggression and flight through repression and emotional insulation are just two of a group of defensive behaviors that we call upon to protect us when we feel threatened. It becomes a vicious cycle. You criticize me so I zap you back, or I retreat and turn away. Then you get angry and I continue to stay mad.

Nobody wins. Everybody loses in the kind of climate that is created by messages which make you defensive. Fortunately, there are preferred responses which build rather than destroy. We will now describe six defense producing patterns of communication and the alternative techniques which make for the warm, comfortable climate that enhances the quality of our lives.

WHAT TO SAY WHEN

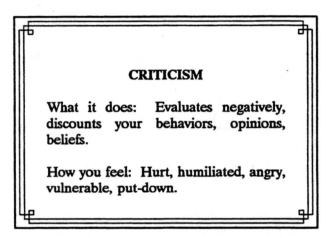

CRITICISM

What it does: Evaluates negatively, discounts your behaviors, opinions, beliefs.

How you feel: Hurt, humiliated, angry, vulnerable, put-down.

CRITICISM

We have implied that criticism creates alienation. But evaluation is a natural response to most situations. We need to be able to say whether or not **KRISPY KRUNCHIES** are bad for your health, or whether or not Mr. Moreno produces on the job. Do you consider Chuck an honest contractor? Has Senator Wiffenbach followed through on his commitment to support school funding? To evaluate, to judge by our own standards, happens to be the way we usually relate to our environment and to the people in it.

However, more often than not, judgment, expressed as criticism, hurts our relationships.

Making negative judgments about others can really sting.
Here are some typical evaluating statements:

> "You'll never get anywhere. You're so disorganized."

> "You're always late. The job must not be important to you."

> "You change your mind 50 times a day. I never know what to believe or do."

> "When I was your age, I had my priorities straight!"

And there are comments that don't point the finger, but nevertheless rankle:

> "That's a peculiar way to set a table."

> "Everyone else responds to my phone messages."

WHAT TO SAY WHEN

"What a messy desk. How can you find
anything!"

We can see that we feel thorned and scorned by
some of these messages. Clearly these kinds of
statements create walls between us. "Fences do
not good neighbors make .. " said the great poet
Frost.

But then again how do you let others know how
uncomfortable you feel when their behaviors
upset you? You address yourself to the *issue*
instead of to the personality. You *describe* the
behavior which upsets you.

WHAT TO SAY WHEN

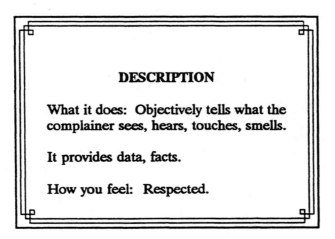

DESCRIPTION

What it does: Objectively tells what the complainer sees, hears, touches, smells.

It provides data, facts.

How you feel: Respected.

The alternative to using an evaluative statement is to describe the offensive situation. We address the behavior or issue rather than the personality. Like the viewer who freezes the action, you can examine and define it for yourself as well as for your partner.

Instead of:	Say:
"Mom, your cooking is boring."	"Foods that aren't spiced don't appeal to me."
"You look so blah! Put on some makeup."	"I don't see color in your cheeks. You

WHAT TO SAY WHEN

	might like wearing blush."
"Bobby, you're so self-ish! You ate all the cookies!"	"I see the cookies are gone, Bobby! Joey tells me he didn't get any."

Description depersonalizes the situation.   You want to change a behavior and not attack or blame.   You don't take an adversarial position when faced with a distressing, threatening situation!

Compare the following:

"Your outfit is so dat-ed!" Don't you ever try anything new?"	"I remember when you bought that dress for Mary's wedding. I think you would look great in the solid colors they're showing now."
"You're so flabby! Peo-ple your age don't have to let themselves go."	"When I see how much weight you've gained, I worry about your health!"
"Can't you ever get to the point instead of giving me a three act play?"	"When I hear so much detail, I lose the point of what you're saying."

WHAT TO SAY WHEN

DESCRIPTION

1.   Use "I" language.
2.   Say what you see.
3.   Be specific.
4.   Don't criticize.

WHAT TO SAY WHEN

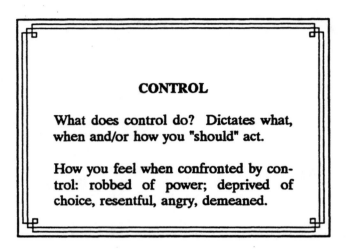

CONTROL

What does control do? Dictates what, when and/or how you "should" act.

How you feel when confronted by control: robbed of power; deprived of choice, resentful, angry, demeaned.

We examined Criticism, the first of six behaviors which arouse defensive responses. A second behavior which makes for a hostile climate is labelled "Control."

"We're going camping this summer."

> "Okay, Fred, you want it that way, we'll do it. If you're so set on camping I guess I'll go. But you know darn well I get tired of cooking. I'd like a *real vacation* this year."

Susie stews in her resentment of Fred's arbitrary, unilateral decision.

WHAT TO SAY WHEN

"The next time you get a parking ticket, no more car. . ."

>   And Jeff knows his dad means it. However,
>   it's likely that Jeff's mental computer process-
>   es: "There he goes again, I'm sick and tired
>   of it. Always ordering me around."

* * *

Memo: "All June vacations canceled."

Your planned time off to go East for your daughter's
graduation is canceled. No ifs, ands or buts! You
helplessly writhe with the decision, because you think
it's arbitrary and unilateral.

For you, it's another put-down. You do what you
have to do, but at a cost to your loyalty to the powers
that be.

* * *

It's a given that most of us become very up-tight when
we feel deprived of the right to make a choice!!
Think about it! How would you feel and respond to
these kinds of statements:

>   "As long as you're in my house, you'll do it
>   my way."

>   "I want to see a movie tonight. We're going
>   to see *Dick Tracy*."

WHAT TO SAY WHEN

"Nobody leaves until this job is finished."

"I'm not going if you're wearing that dress."

Would you feel put-down and resentful? "Yes," you say. But how do you handle the conflict?

Jack Gibb has an option for us! He calls it PROBLEM ORIENTATION.

WHAT TO SAY WHEN

PROBLEM ORIENTATION

What it does: Addresses the needs of each partner.

Asks for input from the other.

How you feel: Challenged as an equal. Respected and valued.

In a conflict situation, remember you're not the only person involved. Acknowledge to your associate that you *share* a problem, and invite *that person* to help you *work it out*! Make a mutual decision-making opportunity.

Instead of:	Say:
"We're going camping this year."	"Jackie, I want to get away from it all and camp this year. I know it's not your bag. Let's talk about it and see what we can work out."

WHAT TO SAY WHEN

"The next time you get a parking ticket, no more car."

"Jim, this is your fourth parking ticket. I'm worried. What's the problem?"

"Cliff, all vacations in June are canceled."

"Cliff, I've been ordered to rescind all leaves in June. I'm sorry. I know you planned to fly east for your kid's graduation. Do you have any suggestions on how to handle this?"

The first controlling approach to the problem represents a unilateral and uncompromising position. "Other" is treated as a non-person. With the second approach, each party's viewpoint is considered.

When faced with a demand, you resent the autocratic indifference to your feelings and needs. On the other hand, with emphasis on the issue as a conflict to be mutually resolved, you can listen and share your views in an open climate of discussion. You may not get what you want, but at least you have a shot in reaching consensus. You feel respected and validated.

WHAT TO SAY WHEN

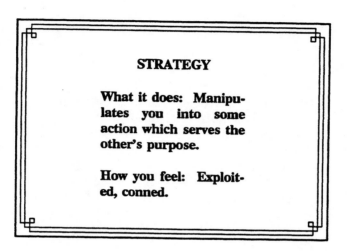

STRATEGY

**What it does: Manipu-
lates you into some
action which serves the
other's purpose.**

**How you feel: Exploit-
ed, conned.**

The self-centered person asks something of you in a
subtle way. Gibb calls this behavior STRATEGY.
The bottom line is that you feel used when the other
manipulates a situation which pressures you to action.

For example, after months of no contact, Susie calls
and chats about her latest adventure. Then she asks
you if you're driving to the Art Fair in Chico; if so,
can you tolerate a passenger? Somehow your warm
energetic responses become rather tepid as you realize
that all Susie wants is some convenient transportation.

WHAT TO SAY WHEN

When your co-worker, after many months of seeming indifference, notices the quality of your reports and approaches you:

> "Harry, your reports are clear and have all the information we need. Have you taken business writing?"

> "Yes, John."

> "Well, I know it's beyond the call of duty, but how about writing up the General Alliance Report for me?"

Did he mention any rewards for you? No! Has he been friendly in the past? No! Understandably, you feel taken in. You're surprised. You can't think fast enough to politely resist the pressure. You swallow hard, and find yourself taking on a project which is demanding. Your hurt and resentment fester. In your mind's eye, next time this guy approaches, you'll run the other way!

Why does this *strategy* elicit a defensive reaction? If you recall, we refer to your sense of self (self-concept) and the omnipresent need to be valued! When you think that other persons want to talk or be with you only to satisfy their needs, you feel demeaned rather than valued, used rather than enhanced!

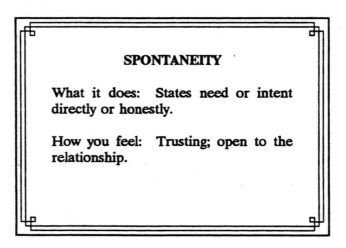

> **SPONTANEITY**
>
> What it does: States need or intent directly or honestly.
>
> How you feel: Trusting; open to the relationship.

How do you avoid putting people on the defensive when you want something from them? We suggest that you make a direct, honest request. Be up front. Don't preface your request with all kinds of flattery or guilt imposing stories. Instead, say what you want!

> "Susy, I need a ride to Chico. I'm calling to find out who has room and wants company! If it's possible, I'd appreciate a ride!"

> "Harry, I'd like you to write up the General Alliance Report. I need to get away and

WHAT TO SAY WHEN

don't have the time. Do you think you can
manage it along with all the other stuff you
have to do? Think about it and let me know."

No hidden agenda here.

We think you'll agree that most of us don't like to
be talked into doing something. We don't like to
feel conned! We'll change the following messages
into spontaneous requests.

Instead of:	Say:
"How would you like to do a favor for me? When you go to the store, pick up some salad fixings?"	"When you go to the store, will you pick up some salad fixings for me?"
"My baby's sick and my mother's visiting from the east all week, and my babysitter didn't show up again. Would you drive the carpool again?"	"I have a problem. I can't take my turn in the carpool today. Can you pick up the kids? I'll take your turn to-morrow."

We're not saying that everybody who asks you to
do something is out to con you. However, we

believe that the modus operandi for some folks is to manipulate us by pressing our guilt, duty and compassion buttons. And when they do, we may respond defensively or suspiciously: "What do they want from me now?" On the other hand, a direct request expressed spontaneously will be more likely to find acceptance.

WHAT TO SAY WHEN

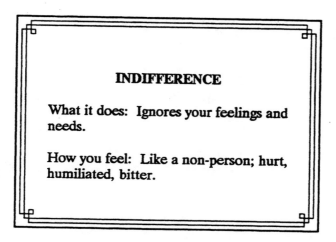

When someone criticizes you it hurts. When you have to dance to another's tune you get unsettled. But sometimes the cruelest nip at your sense of self is when they act as if you're not there! They ignore your space, where you are! Call this behavior *Indifference*.

For example, Debby is worn out because she had just finished finals. She tells her mom how wiped out she feels.

Mom says: "Well, now they're over, you can take me shopping." Talk about <u>cold</u>!

Your husband comes home wearily and speaks of his frustration on the job. You say, "So what else is new?" That's mental cruelty.

These replies cut to the quick. You realize that what's happening to you is not significant to your so-called "significant other."

What you need is an expression of concern and understanding. That's called Empathy.

WHAT TO SAY WHEN

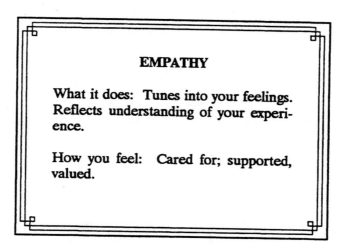

EMPATHY

What it does: Tunes into your feelings. Reflects understanding of your experience.

How you feel: Cared for; supported, valued.

Even though you're busy and taken with many demands, you can show empathy when someone needs you to tune into their feelings.

For example, instead of jumping into what *you* want when your daughter is still reeling from her "finals" traumas, you might say:

> "Debby, you look so tired. I know you've been staying up all night this past

week. Please get some rest! And when
you're feeling human again, how about
taking me shopping?"

And when Davey comes running in with news of
his team's victory, you might say:

"Davey, no wonder you're so excited.
Your team won the game! What was
the score? How did you play? I want
you to tell me all about it as soon as I
can sit down. But first, son, I'm looking
for Debbie. I want to make sure she's
home safe. Do you know where she is?"

And to rewrite the scenario for the husband and
wife, you might hear:

"Oh, Ben, another rough day. It doesn't
change, does it? Come sit down. I've
got dinner ready. We'll talk."

WHAT TO SAY WHEN

Warmth and easy-flowing sharing make for healing and heartening communication. The message is: "Tune in and turn on."

Instead of:

Jackie: I've had it. Cooped up with two sick kids. I'm losing my mind!

Ed: <u>It comes with the territory, Jackie. What's for dinner?</u>

* * *

Joshua: I've been "had" again. The company cut my percentage from 30% to 15% - I can't live on that!

Say:

Jackie: I've had it! Cooped up with two sick kids. I'm losing my mind!

Ed: <u>You've had a real hard day! Can we sit down and talk?</u>

* * *

Joshua: I've been "had" again. The company cut my percentage from 30% to 15% - I can't live on that!

Ellen: <u>I told you to read the contract carefully when you made the terms. By the way, call your sister. She called</u>.

Ellen: <u>What a lousy thing to do. You must be really angry</u>.

It doesn't take much to be empathetic. It takes your willingness and desire to hear another's feelings without judgment. Empathy represents a full measure of your acceptance of that person and where he is.

WHAT TO SAY WHEN

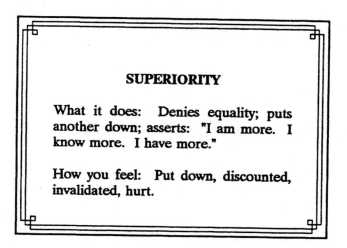

SUPERIORITY

What it does: Denies equality; puts another down; asserts: "I am more. I know more. I have more."

How you feel: Put down, discounted, invalidated, hurt.

The Constitution states that "all men are created equal." But you know that some people are more equal than others. You may be wealthier than I; I may be more skilled at communicating than you. You're prettier than I am. But I can do things with my hands that you envy. There will always be someone more knowledgeable, more skilled, more attractive than you are.

You have enough difficulty coming to terms with what you perceive as your inadequacies. You don't need someone

WHAT TO SAY WHEN

else to tell you how superior they are.   Imagine your
feelings when you hear:

> "Nurse, how can you possibly equate your judgment
> with my medical experience?"

> "I made $10,000 in one stock this year. You took a
> bath, didn't you?"

> "Our division has consistently out-produced yours.
> When are you going to reorganize and get with it,
> Larson?"

> "When I was your age, I was at the top of my class!"

> "I defy anyone to make a better chili than I do."

These messages could generate resentment and anger. The
nurse feels invalidated; the stock customer becomes even
more depressed; the division manager resents the put-down;
the discounted student buckles under the parental bragging,
and the cook turns away, discredited.

In each instance, "superiority" has created a barrier to
further communication. You neither like nor trust this
person who is so ego-centered that he needs to make

WHAT TO SAY WHEN

himself more at your expense. You believe that all men <u>are</u> created equal.

WHAT TO SAY WHEN

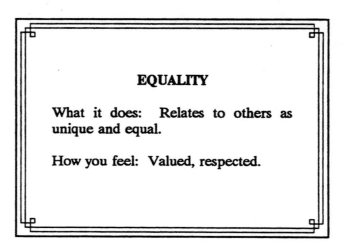

EQUALITY

What it does: Relates to others as unique and equal.

How you feel: Valued, respected.

When we communicate the attitude that we are all equally important, we build trust, show respect and gain a feeling of closeness.

The manager considers the feelings of the nurse's input with respect.

> "Nurse, I've considered your suggestion that Mrs. Wyman's tranquilizers be cut. I am writing orders to decrease gradually. We'll see how she does."

WHAT TO SAY WHEN

The parent acknowledges the child's disappointment:

> "You got a D in math after all that study. You must feel defeated. I remember how hard math was for me."

These messages generate feelings of support and trust. The workers feel respected and part of the team. The students feel esteemed, capable and responsible. The nurse feels validated. The child feels understood and supported.

This attitude brings people together. It says, "I'm OK and you're OK."

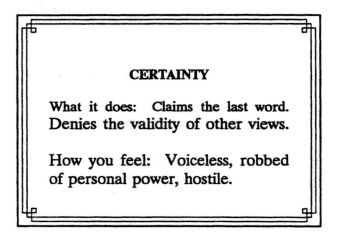

The *know it alls* come on with a vigorous declaration of the *right way* and the *correct thing to do* and the *only path to take*. This certainly leaves no room for argument. The real world is their world. Your perception doesn't count.

> **Jim claims:** "The only path to heaven is to follow the word of the Bible."

Jim's claim doesn't allow your liberal approach to religion.

WHAT TO SAY WHEN

Mary says: "Don't tell me about men. They only want one thing from women!"

Mary's allegation rules out your experiences with men.

* * *

Derek states: "The American car can't come up to the imports."

Your satisfaction with your Lincoln doesn't count with Derek.

* * *

Don declares: "An eye for an eye! Murderers must be put in the electric chair."

All the data you have gathered about capital punishment doesn't hold water for Don.

* * *

Shari argues: "The administration's corruption and dishonesty have set our democracy back 75 years."

Your political views are irrelevant to Shari.

WHAT TO SAY WHEN

When someone comes on so strong that you are left no room to speak your piece, how do you feel? You feel like a non-person. The implication is that your thinking has no value. You feel powerless. Wouldn't you feel hostile to someone who invalidated your self-worth?

You think you have something of value to say. And you want to be recognized.

WHAT TO SAY WHEN

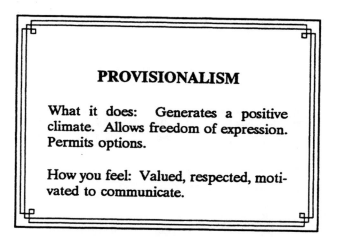

PROVISIONALISM

What it does: Generates a positive climate. Allows freedom of expression. Permits options.

How you feel: Valued, respected, motivated to communicate.

Nobody has all the answers. They say the only certainty is death, taxes and change. When you're aware of the process nature of the life experience, you become more receptive to other ways of being, doing, thinking. Your communication becomes tentative, more *provisional*. You are open to alternatives.

> **Jim says:** "I adhere to the liberal word of the Bible. For me that is the righteous path."

Jim tells you what's right for him. He doesn't claim sole ownership of religious truth.

WHAT TO SAY WHEN

> **Marge says:** "My experience with men has shown me that they only want one thing."

Marge's assertion still gives you the room to share your experience.

* * *

> **Derek states:** "I've owned three import cars and I was happy with them all. I see you just bought another Lincoln. That seems to be your car."

He respects your choice.

* * *

> **Don says:** "I've heard that capital punishment is not a deterrent for murderers. But I voted for capital punishment. I believe in an eye for an eye."

He acknowledges other viable approaches to the issue.

* * *

> **Shari says:** "I don't know how you feel, but for me this administration's contempt for the law has been an abomination!"

She invites your opinion.

Each speaker claims ownership of their ideas. They do not insist that their opinions reflect the "whole truth and nothing but the truth." They're not about to shoot down your opinions. They want to hear what you have to say. They are not closed to difference.

WHAT'S YOUR COMFORT ZONE?

Wherever you are and whenever you speak, your statements create a climate of acceptance or rejection of others. Your messages confirm your perception of another as valued and respected, or disconfirm their judgment and worth.

You can choose to criticize or to describe a difficult situation, to control or to address yourself to the conflict as an equal partner. You can manipulate another person with your hidden agenda or be up front in your transaction. You can play one-upmanship or be equal. You can claim the "last word" or invite another view. The choice is yours. YOU set the climate!

We acknowledge with profound gratitude Jack Gibb's landmark study in which he isolated and categorized these behaviors.

Jack Gibb, "Defensive Communication," Journal of Communication, 11 (1961), pp 141-48.